Kathmandu to Everest

Ryohei Uchida

SBL Springfield Books Limited

Title page photograph: Blue poppy. Atop Mount Lobuje
Above photograph: *Mani* wheels in the outer wall of the Namche *gompa*.

This edition published 1991 by Springfield Books Limited
Norman Road
Denby Dale
Huddersfield
HD8 8TH

First published in the United States 1991 by Chronicle Books

First published in Japan by Yama-Kei Publishers Co., Ltd.
Printed in Japan.

British Library Cataloguing in Publication Data
Uchida, Ryohei
Kathmandu to Everest.
1. Nepal. Travel
I. Title
915.49604

ISBN 0-947655-97-2

Translation: Japan-Michi Interlingual, Inc.
Editing: Judith Dunham
Cover design: Julie Noyes Long
Cover photograph: Ryohei Uchida
Designer: Hikaru Watanabe

CONTENTS

PREFACE

Even if he or she is not able to climb it, any mountain climber would wish to have a close-up look at Mount Everest. In the not-too-distant past, going to the Himalayas was only a dream, but today anyone can go there if they possess a healthy body and a bit of endurance. For a mountain journey in Nepal—we call it trekking—the routes are easy to find, even though they are very high and far away. Accommodations, such as lodges and *bhatti* (teahouses), can be found along the route, and capable guides and porters are available to assist you in your travels.

There are many trekking courses in Nepal. The most popular is the one described in this book, which winds through the villages of the Sherpa tribe, among whom Tibetan Buddhism is widely practiced. This is the course first taken by those pilgrims who suffer from the "Himalayan disease."

Most of the time, trekkers start at Lukla, where the airport is located, but in this book, in consideration of those who travel by bus, we start from Jiri. In addition to the main route, side trips to Thame, Gokyo, and Chhukung are included, and I invite you to explore them.

Even though we use the name Everest Highway, there really is no such road fit to be called a highway. It is a severe course, following a narrow, much-trodden road where local residents travel to and fro, walking through hills and ultimately glacial moraines, where all the while the trekker is exposed to unfamiliar altitudes and cold temperatures.

Discovering the Himalayan landscape is one of the exciting things about trekking, but the most exciting is to make contact with the lives of the local people and their different cultures. In this book, we not only present the scenery encountered along the route but, as much as possible, we also focus on the life of the local people. We hope that the pictures and accompanying articles in this book are useful preparatory knowledge for those who will walk through this course—or, at the very least, that they convey the atmosphere of this special place to those who will not have the opportunity to visit it.

1. From Jiri to Lukla

Jiri–Mali–Shivalaya–Ghatekhola–Deurali–Bhandar–Gholunda–Kinja–Seti–Dhakuchu–Goyam–Lamjura La–Takuto–Junbesi–Thupten Chhulin–Solung–Ringmo–Tragsindho–Manidingma–Phuleli–Jubing–Kharikhola–Kharte–Phuiyan–Surkhe–Lukla

- By bus from Kathmandu, on foot from Jiri

The starting point of the Everest Highway is Jiri, the final stop on an eight-hour bus trip from Kathmandu. From here, it takes about thirteen days to get to the Base Camp. If you fly, the trip takes about seven days starting from Lukla. There is also an airport in Jiri.

Every Saturday a "blue-sky" bazaar is held in Jiri on the east side of the mountain. The villagers are descended from a father who belonged to the Tibetan Kamba tribe and a mother named Jirel, a Sunmar, who are the Nepali gold- and silversmiths.

Let's start trekking from Jiri. Along the way, we can expect to meet various tribal groups.

1 Page 7. What Jiri looks like. From here to the interior, the road narrows to a mere 2 meters (less than 7 feet).
2 The child of a wealthy family being carried on someone's back. Near Mali, transport is dependent on people's backs.
3 Crossing a bridge suspended over Khimti Khola. At Shivalaya, on the other side of the river, is the Solu district where the Sherpa reside.
4 Mother and child of the Chhetri tribe resting at a *bhatti* (teahouse) in Shivalaya. The Chhetri group is the next highest in rank after the Brahman.
5 A man of the Tamang tribe in Shivalaya. Characteristic of this group is the wearing of a *khukri* tucked inside the sash.
6 A Chhetri house in Ghatekhola. The entrance and windows are large. Placed under some of the windows are beehives.
7 & 8 The Dhupachheghi festival, the Sherpa's summer festival in Deurali. Villagers chant "Om mani padme hum!" (O lotus-seated god of the celestial jewel!) while they move clockwise around the altar in front of a monastery.

8

At Deurali, the first large pass, rows of stone *mani* walls inscribed with Buddhist scriptures are lined up one after another. At a hillside basin down from the pass are the Sherpa villages of Changma and Bhandar. From here you walk through the forest country and descend to a small marsh where you reach Gholunda.

The Solu region is a residential area of the Sherpas. In the low grounds along the river, the Baun, the Chhetri, the Rai, and other people live together.

9 Gholunda, at the edge of a small marsh. The river behind the village is Likhu Khola. It is during the rainy season, and the young, green rice and wheat await the October harvest.

10 Baun family in Gholunda. Two girls sit between their grandparents and in front of their mother. They smiled in response to being photographed.

Lamjura La is the largest pass in the Solu district. Kinja, the village where we start, has a name that means "Entrance to the Ascent." From here to the pass runs a sharply angled slope with some stone steps. On the way, we pass such communities as Chinbu (consisting of only a *bhatti* and lodge), Seti, Dhakuchu, and Goyam. At the top of the 3,500-meter-high (11,500-foot-high) pass are *mani* walls, *tar chen* (prayer flags), *laptse* (cone-shaped mounds piled with yak horns and stone plaques inscribed with Buddhist scriptures). Strong winds blow so that even in summer the cold stings the skin.

11 Kinja children. Nepali mountain village children, who cannot watch TV because of the lack of electricity, swing and play at hopscotch. Sometimes, the adults join in.
12 Sherpas in Dhakuchu. A grandmother holds her granddaughter and a mother holds her son. The clothing of Sherpa men and children are not very different from that of other tribes, but the women's aprons, called *matil,* are unique to each tribe.
13 A Sherpa family at a *bhatti* at Goyam. Among the Sherpa, those in the Solu district seem friendlier than those in the Khumbu district. Maybe this is due to a more relaxed attitude resulting from the abundant agriculture.
14 Flowers in the area above Kinja. During the summer rainy season along both sides of the Everest Highway, a variety of flowers bloom profusely.
15 A virgin forest at Lamjura La. At the foot of a Nepali mountain that receives the rains in summer, a rich grove can be seen. Such trees are the villagers' source of energy.

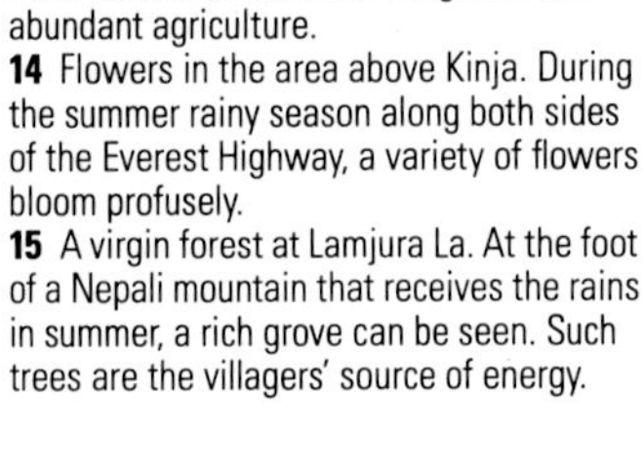

Leaving the main route from Junbesi (discussed on the next page), I like to stop along the way at Thupten Chhulin where a *gompa,* or monastery, is located. Turning to the left along the marsh from Junbesi and climbing for about an hour, we arrive at Thupten Chhulin.

This *gompa* was built in 1959 by priests who escaped their mother country with the fourteenth Dalai Lama, who was exiled to India when anti-Chinese riots occurred in Tibet. The name of the monastery's abbot is Tukche Rinpoche. The *gompa* is set against a backdrop of high mountains, and the priests' small huts are scattered around it. About two hundred people, including nuns and novice priests, live here. This *gompa* received its name from the Dalai Lama himself.

16 The inner yard of the *gompa* at Thupten Chhulin. The buildings are no larger than those at the *gompa* of other villages.
17 Novice priests making dry cheese. Cheese is a precious source of wintertime protein.
18 Priests praying toward the *gompa.* At a place of worship about 100 meters (330 feet) below the *gompa,* priests, nuns, child priests, and young priests all pray by prostrating themselves over and over again, the highest form of prayer in Tibetan Buddhism, when both knees, both elbows, and the head all touch the earth.
19 A nun turning a *mani* wheel while chanting a sutra. In a corner of the dark interior of the shrine, nuns pray intensely for their next lives and for the peace for all humankind.

Spreading throughout the basin of the Junbesi Khola, Junbesi is the biggest village in the Solu district along the Everest Highway. The residents, all of whom are Sherpa, live in about one hundred private houses with their uniquely characteristic white walls. There are two *gompa,* and about five lodges. Entering the village makes us feel that we have indeed come far into the Sherpa heartland.

From Junbesi to Ringmo is a four-hour trek along the hillside road. On the way is the small community of Solung, with about ten houses. The south side is open and bathed in sunshine.

20 A Junbesi Sherpani (woman) sowing barley. In the middle of October, after the summer potato harvest, winter barley is planted in the fields. In the Solung region, barley and potatoes are double-cropped. The lives of these people are relatively well-off.

21 A boy plowing a field. In the divinely influenced activity of agriculture, the roles followed by men and women are clearly determined. Women do very little beyond the sowing. Even though this boy is young, because he is a male, he has a job to do in the fields. The cattle that pull the plow should be male, too. Buffalo, thought to be "messengers of the devil," are taboo and cannot be used.

22 A boy sitting in the doorway of a private house in Solung. Cattle are good friends to children, who name each animal and treat them with affection. Behind the house, part of Junbesi, which we left behind some two hours ago, is visible.

23 The second floor of a private house in Solung. On the first floor are the cattle stable and storehouse. On the second floor is the living area, with a simple bed by the window and a long table nearby.

24 A stove in a private residence in Solung. At a Sherpa house, the east side and / or south side of the second floor usually has a window, and a stove is installed nearby. The room is dim, and the smoke from the fire makes one's eyes sting.

25 Ringmo viewed from Solung. The white-walled residences of Ringmo are scattered on the hillside away from the stream Beni Khola. We are now headed for Tragsindho La, the pass behind the clouds.

26

Tragsindho is a community with only a monastery and some lodges. There is a strong impression of being far away from human habitation. The thickly wooded pass is the last of the three biggest ridges in the Solu region. After a ten-minute descent, a square-shaped *gompa* suddenly appears, and the voice of a priest reciting a sutra is borne to us on the wind.

From Tragsindho, we climb down through a forested area for about two hours and arrive at Manidingma, a large village with three-story houses and the stone-paved roadway unique to such hillside villages. Tamang and Rai groups are mixed together. Among the mixed-tribe villages that lie between Jiri and Lukla, this is the largest.

26 A priest of the Tragsindho *gompa*. His daily routine involves the reading of sutras for four or five hours in a room where the walls are adorned with mandalas and are fitted with shelves for the storage of Buddhist scriptures.
27 A *gompa* scene looking from Tragsindho La pass. Climbing down the hillside behind the *gompa,* we come to Manidingma and Phuleli.
28 The front entrance of the *gompa*. Ornamented gateposts, mossy stone steps, and other details create a unique ambience.
29 The stone pavement of Manidingma. Although stone pavements are often seen at hillside villages, the one in this village is the finest along the Everest Highway.
30 A Rai tribeswoman putting the laundry out to dry. There is no designated place for drying clothes at the houses in these mountain villages. The women take advantage of any sunny place, including benches and woodpiles.

27

28

29

30

Climbing down a trail through the hillside farming fields for about an hour from Manidingma, we arrive at Phuleli, a small Rai community. This is exactly halfway to the Dudh Kosi. Departing Ringmo or Tragsindho in the morning, you can arrive here in time for lunch. The Rai who operate a *bhatti* here amiably offered us an oven so that we could prepare our food. To entertain the visitors from afar, they played Nepali music on a radio that was turned up so loud it made our ears ring.

After we crossed the waters of the Dudh Kosi and ascended a bit, the grass-roofed houses of Jubing appeared within an area that looks like a low-altitude temperate zone.

31, 32 & 33 Rai girls in Phuleli. Among all Nepali women, Rai tribeswomen seem to wear the most accessories on their faces. They hang big rings from their earlobes and insert *phuri* in their nostrils. The most characteristic ornament is a *bulaki,* hung under the nose. The young woman in photo 31 wears her best clothing, and the other photos show girls in typical daily garb.
34 A Rai mother standing in her doorway holding her child. The watch on her left wrist is the latest in accessories.
35 A Rai house in Jubing. Note the grass roof and mezzanine style. Along the mountainside behind this house lies Kharikhola.
36 Crossing, with trepidation, a perilous, temporary bamboo bridge spanning the Dudh Kosi. In the summer of 1985, a glacial lake deep in the Thame region overflowed, and most of the suspension bridges over both Bhote Kosi and Dudh Kosi were washed away.

36

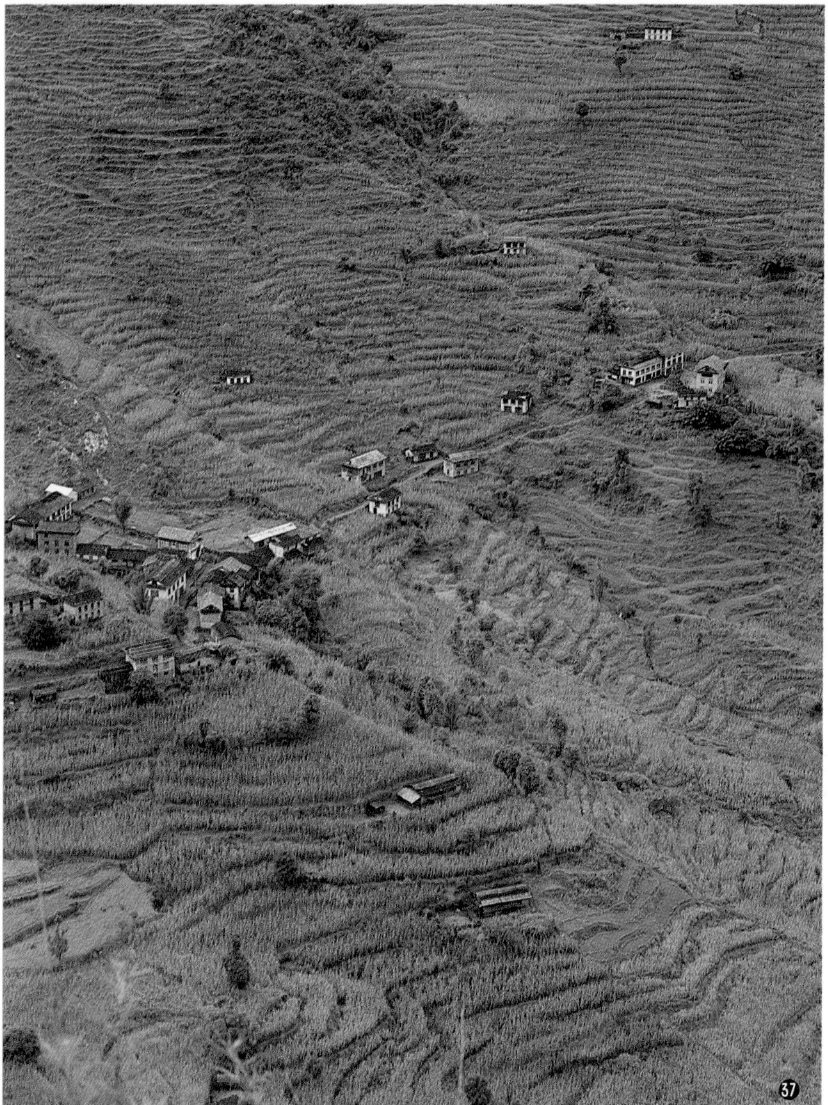

Kharikhola has about eighty buildings. The terraced farmlands reach up the hillside, as if for the heavens. This area is the upper limit of the rice harvest along the Dudh Kosi basin. About twenty buildings are crowded together in the village center. Several of these buildings—a lodge, a shop dealing in daily necessities *(pasal)*, and a tailor shop *(damai)*—resemble a bazaar.

From Kharte, to the north, we proceed through the forested area lying a few hundred meters (about a thousand feet) higher up and cross through Khari La, the pass on the border between the Solu and Khumbu districts. In front of us lies Phuiyan. During this stretch, we encounter the most uninhabited area along the entire Everest Highway. From June to September, mountain leeches abound. Descending to the end of the forest zone, we reach the valley village of Surkhe, located just below the Lukla airport.

37 The Highway as it runs through terraced farmlands of Kharikhola. The area crowded with houses is the center of the village. The tin-roofed building is an elementary/middle school.

38 A *bhatti* in Phuiyan. There are forty houses in the area where the forest land was clearcut. Proceeding from Phuiyan, we come to the Khumbu district. One summer evening, this *bhatti* was crowded with travelers escaping the falling rain.

39 A wooden bridge in Surkhe. In Nepali mountain villages, suspension bridges generally are used for large rivers, and wooden bridges for small rivers. The family living at one side of the bridge maintains a lodging facility. Two roads diverge here: a sharply sloping road that runs from the bridge to Lukla, where the airport is located, and an old road that heads into the interior through Chaumrikharka.

2. From Lukla to Namche Bazar

Lukla–Chapling–Kyomma–Chumlo–Ghat–Phakding–Benkar–Chumoa–Monjo–Jorsale–Namche Bazar

- Flying in from Kathmandu, on foot from Lukla

2

Lukla became the entrance to the Everest Highway when it was connected with Kathmandu by air. Around the airport, not only the Sherpa but also the Rai, the Tamang, and the Magar have started to manage lodges and *bhatti.* Previously, Lukla was a village with about a dozen buildings, but now there are over a hundred. Every Thursday there is a bazaar, even though it cannot be compared with the one in Namche Bazar.

Because most of the trekkers who aim for the Everest Highway make use of the air transportation available, they take their first steps from Lukla.

1 Page 23. To create the Lukla airport, about 400 meters (1,300 feet) of the southern slope was leveled. Sixteen-passenger Twin Otters service the area.
2 Chaumrikharka and the old highway. The road that stretches below Lukla was the major highway before the airport was built. Currently, however, few use it.
3 Bazaar in Lukla. Commodities for sale include rice, wheat flour, and raw buffalo meat. There are only about fifty dealers, and the number of buyers is still small, but the signs point to continued growth.
4 A young Sherpani hired as a porter. She is waiting for departure near the 30-kilo (66-pound) load assigned to her.
5 People enjoying a game of billiards. Airport workers who came into some free time due to the cancellation of a flight bet on a kind of desk billiards game called carom board.
6 A Magar mother and her children. The mother helps her children groom themselves.
7 A child delighting in playing airplane. Pretending to be an airplane by holding a bamboo pole between his legs, he soars around the street.
8 A Rai family, photographed at Chopling. Having sold their products at Namche Bazar, they return bearing their empty bamboo baskets.

3

4

5

6

7

8

10

11

12

13

It takes only four hours to go from Lukla to Phakding. To the eyes of those who arrive at Lukla by air, the land of the Sherpas and everything in it are fresh and new. Representations of Tibetan Buddhism can be seen on the way to Phakding, and along the road run long stone fences that keep the cattle from intruding. When we descend to the riverbank from the mountain pass stretching along the Dudh Kosi, we come to Phakding.

9 A private residence in Kyomma. Many of the roofs of ordinary private residences like this one are made of wood and bamboo mats weighted down with heavy stones. The roofs on the houses in Namche Bazar are being converted to galvanized steel. *Tar chen,* banners for protection against evil, flutter in the wind.
10 A huge rock inscribed with Buddhist scripture stands at the outskirts of Ghat village. A Tibetan scripture reads "Om mani padme hum!" (O lotus-seated god of the celestial jewel!).

11 Cattle crossing a wooden bridge in Chumlo. Cattle, rather than horses, are the pack animals of the Khumbu area. Although slow moving, they do not waste any time on the road and usually arrive at their destinations before the people do.
12 Near Phakding. During the summer rainy season, flowers bloom between the rocks of the fence. The greenery is stunning.
13 The kitchen of a *bhatti* in Phakding. Because wood is used for fuel, kitchen utensils become black with smoke. Here, you can order *dhalu bhat,* a staple food of the Nepali diet, and noodles.

14

From Phakding to Benkar, we thread forward at a higher altitude on a road that winds through a natural forest of pines and cedars along the right bank of the Dudh Kosi. Above this narrow road is a rock wall and below it is a cliff. The distance to the opposite bank narrows to 80 meters (260 feet).

Behind Benkar run rock walls, and in their quiet shadows stand a dozen or so residences. Far up the valley, the snowy peak of 6,623-meter-high (21,856-foot-high) Thamserku juts out.

From Lukla airport, 6,011-meter-high (19,836-foot-high) Kwangde and parts of the Rolwaling Mountains can be seen. Also, from Chumlo, the 5,579-meter-high (18,410-foot-high) west peak of Kusum Kanguru can be surveyed. From Benkar, ever grander mountains appear, heightening our sense of the trekking experience.

14 A *mani* stone in Benkar. *Mani* means "jewel" in Sanskrit. In the distance shines the peak of Thamserku.

15 A community in Benkar. Located on the right bank of the Dudh Kosi, Benkar receives sunlight in the early morning, which melts the thin veneer of ice from roofs and roads. In another two weeks or so, the year's first snow will fall. To the right of center can be seen the large *mani* stone pictured in photo 14.

16 Crossing the holy river, the Dudh Kosi. Nepali, especially the mountain-dwelling Sherpa, seem to harbor a strong fear of rivers and lakes. In particular, when crossing this type of bridge, they move cautiously, step-by-step, praying to the water gods.

15

16

Crossing over to the right bank of the Dudh Kosi on the outskirts of Benkar, we climb up a little, passing Chumoa. As the area around us opens up, we arrive at Monjo, somewhat relieved from the hemmed-in feeling that had been oppressing us.

Here, at a field office of the Sagarmatha National Park, the entrance fee is collected.

When we cross a large suspension bridge and take the road along the left bank, Jorsale lies ahead. From here, the gorge-shaped entrance to the ascent to Namche Bazar presents itself. Only 50 meters (165 feet) separate the river's banks, and it is the narrowest section of the Highway.

17 A street lined with rock walls in Monjo. On both sides are fields of potatoes, wheat, and other crops. After harvest, the fields become a campground. Looming over the white-walled houses unique to the Sherpa towers the 5,761-meter-high (19,011-foot-high) holy mountain of Khumbila.
18 A private residence in Monjo. The outer wall is constructed by carefully piling pieces of stone to a thickness of some 40 centimeters (16 inches). Clay is daubed over both inside and outside, and the whole is painted white with lime.
19 Jorsale. The Highway proceeds through a small flat area sandwiched between mountain and river. Jorsale is a village at the bottom of the valley where a dozen residences are lined up along the road.
20 Part of a *mendan* in Monjo. *Mendan* refers to a long wall with *mani* stones piled up along the side of the road. This village's *mendan* is well preserved and beautiful. When people pass by such symbols of Tibetan Buddhism, they walk to the left.

3. Namche Bazar

Namche Bazar

1

Sited 3,364 meters (11,101 feet) above sea level, Namche Bazar is the heart of the Khumbu region and is called the hometown of the Sherpa. Two- and three-story houses and lodges are crowded together in the horseshoe-shaped basin, surrounded on three sides by hills and open to the south. On every roof, prayer banners flutter in the wind. So many people live in this high-altitude town because of the abundant source of fresh water and the regularly held bazaar. The surrounding villages have farmland and *kharka* (summer pasture) and are almost self-contained, but this village is not so blessed. The people in Namche Bazar support themselves by working as guides or by making use of their business abilities.

1 Page 31. *Chorten* in Namche Bazar. This tower made of stones and clay is identical to the stupa of ancient India. Inside, Buddhist scriptures and gems are stored. It is also said to be the tomb of a high priest.
2 View of the village, with private residences built as if on steps up the hillside. There are many sloped roads with stone fences. Because of the altitude, visitors quickly feel short of breath when they climb up to the village.
3 A group of private residences and 6,011-meter-high (19,836-foot-high) Kwangde. The morning light, which illuminates the mountains first, at last has descended into the village. As the temperature rises, another day begins for the village folk.
4 Sherpa dance. The summer rainy season is the villagers' off-season, when they recuperate from their spring labors and prepare themselves for the coming autumn activities. This four-day festival—called *fa-ngi*—unfolded on the eastern hills. The opening act was a Sherpa dance by gaily dressed men and women.
5 Inside a *bhatti*. The tea served in this village has a different taste from that in other villages, probably due to the delicious spring water. The tea served by this Sherpani was excellent.

Every Saturday, a "blue-sky" bazaar is held on the crest of the eastern hills. Over a hundred sellers—Tamang and Rai, who live near the lower reaches of the Dudh Kosi—are present. The purchasers number up to five hundred Sherpas, who come from the surrounding villages including Namche Bazar, Khumjung, Khumde, Thame, Tengboche, Phortse, and Pangboche. The merchandise, contained in a bamboo basket called a *roko,* consists mainly of staple foodstuffs like rice, wheat, corn, and *kodo* (a kind of millet). Also sold at the market are everyday essentials such as tea, sugar, and petroleum, carried on people's backs along the Everest Highway from Kathmandu. The hour between nine and ten o'clock is the most crowded time and abounds with excitement.

6 A bazaar scene. On a narrow, terraced hilltop, buyers and sellers jostle each other during the peak period, from nine to ten o'clock.
7–12 Buyers and sellers at the bazaar. Since the commodities do not have price tags, purchasers first must ask the price, then bargain. The facial expressions of both parties change, and clamorous wrangling is carried on amid furious gesticulation. Once the negotiation is complete, item and money are exchanged with peaceful expressions. Dealing in many commodities, the sellers use brass vessels such as the *mana* in photo 10 and the *pathi* in photo 11, and sales are conducted according to cost per measure.

13

The Sherpa are very religious. Whenever they have the time, they chant "Om mani padme hum!" (O lotus-seated god of the celestial jewel!). They are said to repeat this chant as many as a thousand times each day. Chanting as many sutra's as possible is believed to be a virtuous deed that will influence the next life. Young Sherpa and the guides used by trekkers and climbing groups chant silently. When they visit a *gompa,* they repeatedly prostrate themselves before the object of veneration. They never fail to show respect when they pass by religious symbols, and believe that the gods are always present in the earth, water, fire, wind, and sky.

13 An aged couple reading sutra. When a passage is read, the wife sitting behind her husband counts one bead along the rosary.
14 *Mani* wheels on the outside of a *gompa.* When people pass by the *mani* wheels, they turn the cylinder-shaped objects clockwise while chanting sutra. It is said that one rotation has the same virtuous effect as chanting a sutra one thousand times.
15 Old wooden *mani* wheels. As seen in photo 14, the old wooden wheels are gradually being replaced by red copper ones.
16 *Cho tar* and *chorten. Cho tar* are prayer banners for the gods, blockprinted with sutra. The five colors at the top of each banner symbolize, from the top down, sky, wind, fire, water, and earth.
17 & 18 Masks used by dancers. Inside the *gompa,* a dozen different kinds of masks are displayed.
19 Morning prayers, diligently conducted, at the *gompa.* A horn sounds at dawn, and the priests commence to read the sutra. As the morning sun shines into the shrine, the gods of the mandala on the walls seem to awaken.

14

15

16

19

17

18

The lively village of Namche Bazar is the heart of the Khumbu district. From here, the Everest Highway and the roads to Thame and Gokyo diverge. Various facilities, mainly three-story lodges and restaurants, are available. Travelers headed to the interior regions pass through this village. In 1985, the village's self-governing organization decided to build a power station, the first for any of the local towns. When the electric lights began to be lit from five to ten o'clock in the evening, the lives of the villagers sustained a sea change. Every hour a bell in the village chimes out the time.

20 Pages 38 and 39. A night view of Namche Bazar. Lights glow brightly from within the local residences and lodges. For the residents, the electricity is like a gift from the gods. At 5:30 p.m. on an autumn evening, 6,623-meter-high (21,856-foot-high) Thamserku rises behind the village, catching the setting sun.
21 A distant view of Everest. The top of the eastern hills is a good place from which to view the mountains. Visible are 6,501-meter-high (21,453-foot-high) Taweche, to the left, and 6,812-meter-high (21,480-foot-high) Ama Dablam, to the right. In the center can be seen the grand 8,516-meter-high (28,102-foot-high) peak of Lhotse. To its left, 8,848-meter-high (29,028-foot-high) Everest reveals its countenance.
22 Snow-covered Namche Bazar at the end of December. During the night, the village was covered by a snowfall about 2 meters (6½ feet) deep. The mountain in the distance is 6,367-meter-high (21,011-foot-high) Kusum Kanguru. The east peak is the high one.
23 Trekkers following the line of the cliff near Sanarsa. As the Highway continues beyond Namche Bazar, some parts are hazardous, with a sheer rock face above and a steep precipice below. The trekkers walk on, constantly looking up at the high peaks ahead of them.

4. From Namche Bazar to Thame

(Side Trip)

Namche Bazar–Phurte–Tesho–Thamo–Tumde–Thame

2

For those who can afford to spend extra time around Namche Bazar, the journey to Thame makes a good side trip. The road to Thame is a trade route to Tibet and passes over Nangpa La. Along the way, we pass through the villages of Phurte, Tesho, Thamo, Thomde, and Tumde, where we find a large number of *chorten* and *mendan*. Surrounded by mountains, they make for wonderful pictures. Because so few travelers visit this area, the local people exhibit a certain ingenuousness. The wind blowing from Thame brings with it the smell of Tibet.

1 Page 41. A view of Phurte and the peak of Thamserku. Proceeding west from Namche Bazar for about an hour, we arrive at Phurte, above the Bhote Kosi, whose headwaters are at Nangpa La. A *chorten* stands at the entrance to a two-story lodge.
2 A *chorten* in Thamo. In every village, *chorten* stand by the side of the road. The *chorten* in Thamo are especially large, and they harmonize well with the distant peak of Thamserku.
3 A view overlooking Thamo. There are about eighty buildings and, on the hillside, a *gompa*. Terraced fields spread over the mountains. The road to Thame does not have as many sharp ups and downs as the Everest Highway.
4 A private residence in Thamo. Although this residence looks no different from Sherpa houses in other villages, it is rare to see futons put out to dry in the autumn sunshine.
5 The Thamo *gompa*. The size of a *gompa* seems to be determined by a village's financial status. This village's *gompa* is not very large.

3

4

5

6

Thame is about 200 meters (650 feet) above the Bhote Kosi. At a flat sandy place lined by ***byakusing*** (a kind of juniper), the Sherpa holy tree, private residences spread out, and a kind of deserted atmosphere drifts about. Potatoes, harvested in July and August, are the major product of the village. Other than potatoes, only ***kodo,*** a kind of millet, can be harvested. The higher the land, the more limited the quality and quantity of agricultural crops, resulting in a poorer diet. Among the Sherpa villages there is a hierarchy, and Thame seems to be regarded as inferior to Namche Bazar.

6 A Sherpani in the kitchen of a private residence in Thame. The ovens in the kitchens of Sherpa houses are made of iron or clay. In Thame, there are more Tibetan-style iron ovens.
7 A *bhatti* hostess twirling her *mani* wheel. While chanting sutra, she twirls the wheel and counts the turns on the prayer beads in her left hand. These rosaries, primarily Buddhist holy articles, are also used as calculating devices. The metal plates arrayed on the shelf in the background are dinnerware called *deluman.*
8 A family viewed on the street. When I positioned the camera to take the photograph, these children, who at first looked at me as if seeing something exotic, nearly started to cry, but they were soothed by their grandmother.
9 Children sticking their heads out a second-floor window. I may have seemed unusual to them, which means visitors are rare in Thame.

On the way from Thame to Trashi Laptsa, a *gompa* stands under a large wall of rock on a small, high hillside. Around the *gompa,* priests' residences and a dozen or so private homes are built on terraces, which form an upper village in contrast with the lower one. The number of priests here is as small as a dozen, but priests coming over Nangpa La from Tibet never fail to stop here.

10 Private residences in Thame and the Rolwaling Mountains. The land around the private houses appears to be sandy, but in the summer becomes a potato field carpeted in green. A *gompa* can barely be seen on the hillside to the right. From the recesses of the valley, snowy mountains, such as (from the right) 6,730-meter-high (22,209-foot-high) Pigphera Go Shar, 6,696-meter-high (22,096-foot-high) Panayo Toppa, and 6,500-meter-high (21,450-foot-high) Teng Kangpoche, are visible.
11 Thame scene with *chorten.* The view from the *gompa* is superb. Right below is a *chorten,* and above the hills toward Namche Bazar are 6,685-meter-high (22,060-foot-high) Kang Taiga, on the left, and 6,623-meter-high (21,856-foot-high) Thamserku, on the right.
12 Inside the *gompa.* A richly colored world with Buddhist scriptures stored on the shelves, a precious parasol hanging from the ceiling, and mandala painted on the walls appeared in the light of the camera's flash.
13 The *gompa* in Thame. A closer view of the *gompa* in the background of photo 10. The white-walled houses behind the *gompa* are priests' residences and ordinary private houses. Thame consists of an upper village, whose center is the *gompa,* and a lower village spread out across a sandy patch of ground.
14 Page 48. A view overlooking the lower village. On the terraced hillside by the Thame Khola, which flows down from Trashi Laptsa, spread out farmland and private residences enclosed by stone fences.

13

5. Khumjung

Khumjung

1

2

Khumjung, at 3,790 meters (12,507 feet) above sea level, spreads out over the beautiful southern slope of the 5,761-meter-high (19,011-foot-high) holy mountain of Khumbila in the Khumbu district. There are about eighty buildings, a little fewer than at Namche Bazar, and they cover a wide area. The Hillary School was built by Sir Edmund P. Hillary for elementary, middle, and high school students from Khumjung and surrounding villages.

Many *kharka* (summer pastures) lie along the Gokyo route. Khumde, to the west of Khumjung, has the only hospital in the Khumbu region, also built by Hillary. The people of Khumde have the right to use the *kharka* located above Pheriche, which is along the Everest Highway.

1 Page 49. A view looking down over Khumjung from Tengboche. The private residences and farmlands that spread throughout the intermontane basin can be viewed from afar. In the upper area is the neighboring village of Khumde. The mountains in the distance are the Rolwaling.
2 An old woman and her grandchild relaxing in the sunshine. While humming "Om mani padme hum!" (O lotus-seated god of the celestial jewel!), she turns her *mani* wheel and counts her beads.
3 Houses in Khumjung. In the vivid green fields during the summer grow buckwheat and *kodo,* a kind of millet.
4 A square *chorten* in the outer village area. *Chorten* are usually round, so a square-shaped one seems unusual, though square *chorten* can be seen in Tengboche as well.
5 *Mendan.* A long narrow wall contains stones inscribed with Buddhist scriptures. When people encounter a *mendan,* they have to pass to its left.
6 Pages 52 and 53. The peaks of Ama Dablam during the rainy season. Shrouded in fog and mist, Ama Dablam floats as if in a *sumi* painting.

3

4

5

The mountains that can be seen from Khumjung are, on the east, 6,812-meter-high (22,480-foot-high) Ama Dablam and 6,685-meter-high (22,060-foot-high) Kang Taiga; on the west, the Rolwaling Mountains; and to the north, the 5,761-meter-high (19,011-foot-high) Sherpa holy mountain of Khumbila. The snowmelt of Khumbila becomes the fountain waters of Namche Bazar.

7 Snowy Khumjung on a sunny day with Ama Dablam in the distance. Ama means "mother," and Dablam means "star-shaped pendant," such as those worn by formally dressed Sherpani. Within the pendant is kept a small figure of Buddha.
8 *Chorten* and the holy mountain of Khumbila. Khumjung is the first village in the Khumbu region where many *chorten* are located. The large, handsome chorten here are topped with metal embellishments. From our visit, we sensed the wealth and deep religiosity of the villagers.
9 Page 56. Kang Taiga (on the left) and Thamserku (on the right). Khumjung, blessed with expanses of arable land, has long stone fences to prevent cattle from intruding on the fields. Kang Taiga means "saddle of snow."

6. From Khumjung to Gokyo

(Side Trip)

Khumjung–Moung La–Phortse Tenga–Dole–Luza–Machhermo–Panka–Gokyo

1

2

3

4

5

The Gokyo route, which is as popular as the main highway, takes three days for a one-way trip from Khumjung.

Going from Khumjung to Moung La, we follow the hillside on the left bank of the Dudh Kosi's main course, passing through such *kharka* as Dole, Luza, Machhermo, and Panka, and enter the ablation valley of Ngojumba (a basin between a glacier and a hillside). Going past two glacial lakes, and arriving at a third, Dudh Pokhari, at last we come to Gokyo. There are fewer ups and downs, compared with the main Highway, so walking is relatively easy.

1 Page 57. A *chorten* at Moung La pass. There is a fine view from this pass. Behind the *chorten* is the hill where Tengboche is located. To the left rises Ama Dablam.
2 Phortse as seen from Moung La. After we clear the gentle slope of a wide ridge, we see the private residences and farm fields. The villagers are accustomed to using any available flat land.
3 The Sherpa holy tree. Called *byakusing,* it is, along with the *kurusing* tree, a kind of birch, the holy tree of the Sherpa.
4 The Dudh Kosi and the peaks of Kang Taiga and Thamserku. This river, whose source is the Ngojumba Glacier snowmelt, is the Sherpa holy river. Dudh means "milk," and Kosi means "river." The village sitting on the middle of the mountain slope is Phortse.
5 Dole *kharka*. Neither people nor cattle can be seen in this *kharka*. Only the vivid green of fresh pasture grass spreads over the field.
6 Luza *kharka*. Growing pasture grass for the winter is the summertime job in the *kharka*. Consequently, all pasturelands are enclosed by stone fences to prevent intrusion by the cattle.
7 Upper section of the Luza *kharka*. We passed three Sherpani porters coming back from Gokyo, stepping lightly toward Luza *kharka*.
8 A mother and her children heading toward Gokyo. This mother and her children, heading toward Gokyo from Khumjung, caught up with us near Panka *kharka*. The toddler was proceeding indefatigably. A baby was sleeping in the bamboo basket that the mother carried on her back.

6

7

8

Gokyo, a ***kharka*** lying at the far end of this side trip, is 4,750 meters (15,675 feet) above sea level. Seven barns are scattered on the eastern shore of Dudh Pokhari (Milk Lake), called Tso Rangma in the Sherpa language. Around June, when the monsoons have started, families come up to the ***kharka*** from the villages with their livestock. They work hard, milking the animals both morning and evening to make butter and cheese. In early September, they cut the pasture grass and store it in their barns. Then they return to their villages with dairy products as presents.

9 Pages 60 and 61. A Gokyo scene. The entire pasturage has blossomed into a field of flowers, shining with sunlight after a rain. The mountain behind Dudh Pokhari is part of the mountain range separating Dudh Kosi and Bhote Kosi. The peak has no name.
10 Flowers blooming at the water's edge. These flowers bloom in a marshland that runs through an ablation valley, a sunken area that stretches between a glacier and a hillside. The 8,201-meter-high (27,063-foot-high) Cho Oyu, visible in the distance, is whiter now than during other seasons because of the snowfalls of the rainy season.
11 Mother and child in the *kharka.* During the summer, it rains every day. Once in a while the sun peeps out, lasting at the most a couple of hours. A young mother lets her firstborn daughter, only eight months old, enjoy the brief sunlight in the grasslands.
12 Baking potato bread. People eat bread seasoned with *khursani,* a mixture of cheese, salt, hot peppers, and garlic. Along with boiled potatoes, it constitutes the main food of the Sherpa.
13 An overview of Dudh Pokhari and Gokyo *kharka* from halfway up Gokyo Peak. Above the lake lies Ngojumba Glacier.
14 Churning milk. In the *kharka,* everyone wakes up early and makes butter and cheese by churning the milk taken that morning and the evening before. Then they eat breakfast.
15 Yaks crossing Dudh Pokhari. Yaks that have been milked are driven to the mountainside on the lower reaches of Gokyo Peak.

13

14

15

The view from 5,483-meter-high (18,094-foot-high) Gokyo Peak could be even better than the view from Kala Pattar. Nearby to the north, a great "folding screen" of high mountains stands in line: from the left, Cho Oyu, Ngojumba Kang, and Gyachung Kang. To the east, from the left, Everest, Nuptse, Lhotse, and even Makalu can be seen. Under the feet of the trekker lies 1-kilometer-wide and 16-kilometer-long (½-mile by 9½-mile) Ngojumba Glacier. The scene of an ablation valley holding three glacial lakes can be viewed here.

16 Ngojumba Glacier and Dudh Pokhari from Gokyo Peak. Glacial lakes and side moraines can be seen, and the structure of the glacial zone can be easily understood. From the left, the mountains are Taweche, Kang Taiga, and Thamserku, averaging 6,000 meters (19,500 feet) in height.
17 Southeast view from Gokyo. At the left side of the picture, in the distance, is 8,463-meter-high (27,928-foot-high) Makalu. At the right are Taweche, and, to its left, Cholotse.
18 Gyachung Kang, in the center, and 7,646-meter-high (25,232-foot-high) Ngojumba Kang II summit, as seen from Gokyo Peak.
19 Cho Oyu and Dudh Pokhari. Above the lake, Cho Oyu, meaning "God of the Turquoise Jewel," scatters clouds of snow. On the right are Ngojumba Kang I and II summits.
20 Page 66. Toward Everest from Gokyo. On the left is the pyramid-shaped mountain of 8,848-meter-high (29,028-foot-high) Everest. The camel-humped mountain is Nuptse, and the rock peak behind it is Lhotse. On the right is the triangular summit of Makalu.

17

18

19

7. Tengboche

Tengboche

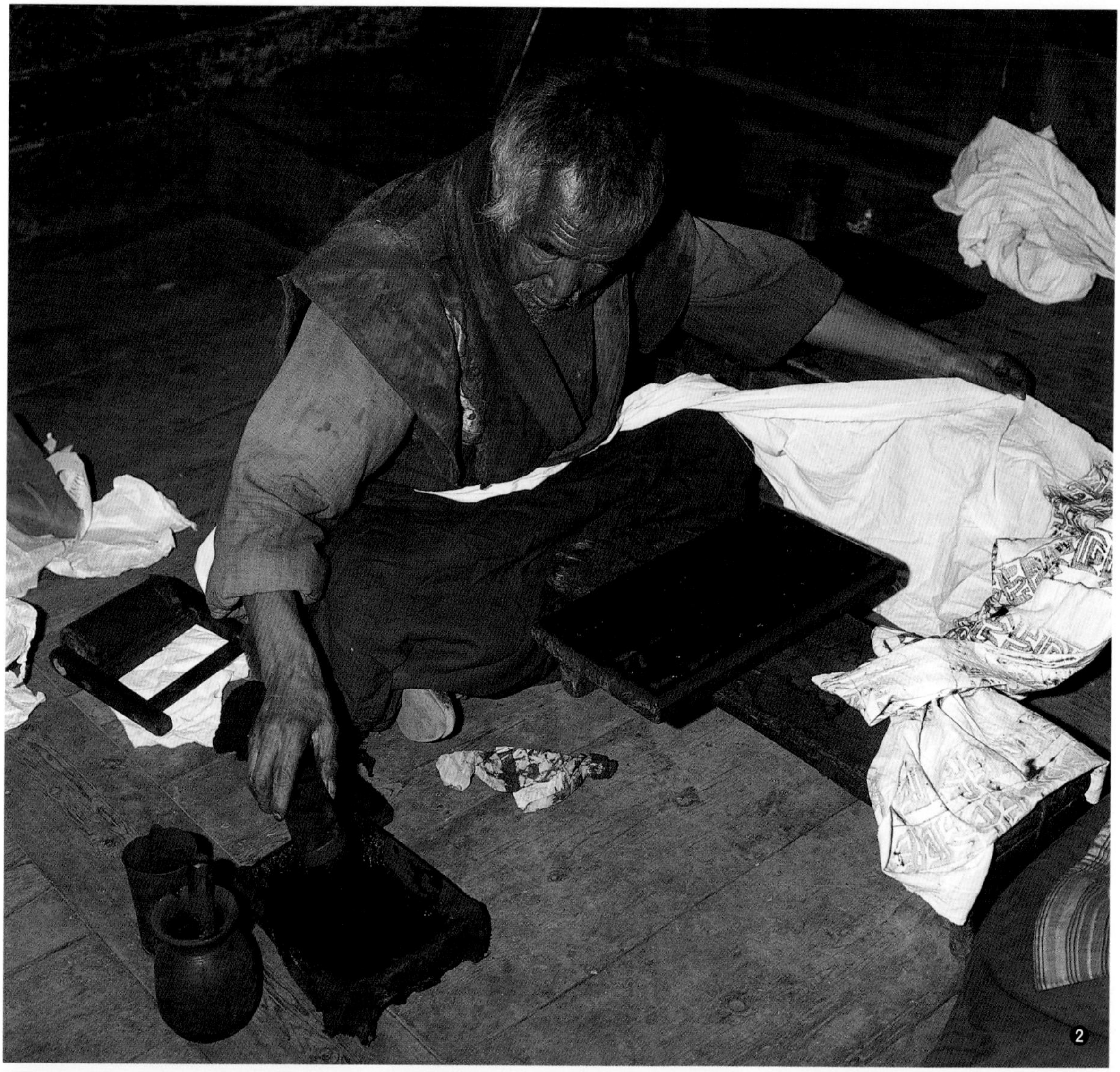
2

3

4

5

At 3,867 meters (12,761 feet) above sea level, Tengboche is located atop a hill, the view from which is spectacular. Not quite a village, Tengboche has only a *gompa,* which serves as the Khumbu district's chief temple of a particular sect of Tibetan Buddhism. This old Nyingma sect was founded by Padmasambhava. Master Nawong Tenzen Jangpo Rinpoche is from Namche Bazar, and the priests are also Sherpa from the surrounding villages. Everyone lives at the *gompa.* Usually, *gompa* are built against mountains or rock walls. This *gompa,* however, stands on a spacious plateau. The main temple was completely destroyed by an electrical fire in January 1989 and is under reconstruction.

1 Page 67. Tengboche *gompa* and 6,812-meter-high (21,480-foot-high) Ama Dablam. The view from Tengboche is excellent. To the left of Ama Dablam, 8,516-meter-high (28,102-foot-high) Lhotse and 7,855-meter-high (25,922-foot-high) Nuptse can be seen. Beyond them, Mount Everest juts up into the sky.
2 A temple craftsman creates woodblock prints of Buddhist scriptures on *tar chen* banners.
3 The main temple of the *gompa* glowing in the evening sun.
4 Three Buddhist statues facing the entrance to the first floor of the main temple. At the center sits Amida, called Jo Rinpoche. To his left is a bodhisattva named Chenrezik, and to his right is Padmasambhava, the founder of Nyingma, who is called Guru Rinpoche (Most Valued Treasure Master).
5 *Mani* wheels in the temple. When one leaves the *gompa,* it is customary to take a clockwise walk around the main temple. At that time, it is said, turning the *mani* wheels results in an increase in virtue.
6 A mural on the second floor of the main temple. Depicted is Padma Hbyun Gneas, one of the eight transformations of Padmasambhava. It is a drawing of the elucidation of the Supreme Yoga Tantra to Mandarava, the daughter of the King of Sohoru.
7 *Thanka,* a Buddhist painting, hanging on the first floor. On the left is a wrathful manifestation called Khro Bohi Sha Tshogo, and on the right is one of the thirty-five *tathagata.* Penitents acknowledge their sins and wrongdoings and, in a spirit of repentance, confess to the *thanka.*
8 A mandala drawn on the ceiling. A mandala is a Buddhist painting representing the divine infinite on the basis of Tantric philosophy. Many mandala are painted throughout the temple.

6

7

8

In Tengboche, for three days following the day of October's full moon, a fourteen-scene masked dance drama, inspired by Tibetan Buddhism, called a *mani rimdu,* is held. During the day of the full moon, a memorial service, or *rilbu,* is conducted on behalf of various holy figures, in the outdoor festival grounds on the west side of the *gompa.* From the morning following the full moon until that evening, a dance drama, called *cham* in Tibetan and *mani rimdu* in Nepali, is acted out in the *gompa* yard. Then, on the evening of the third day, a ceremony called *jinsa,* where firewood is burned on a sand mandala, concludes the festival. The first performance of the *mani rimdu* in Tengboche was in 1930.

9 The opening of the dance drama. Before the first scene, a ceremony, called *rol mo,* is held by eight priests clanging cymbals. Here, the first two priests appear.
10 The *rilbu* memorial service. Chanting is conducted while several hundred people from neighboring villages, as well as tourists, watch. The Rinpoche can be seen in the building on the left.
11 Prelude to the *rilbu.* Before chanting, a prelude played on several musical instruments continues for about ten minutes.
12 From *gompa* to *rilbu* festival grounds. Following the line of leading priests, a musical ensemble, led by horns called *dun chen,* precedes the Rinpoche.
13 The concluding fire ceremony. At four o'clock in the afternoon of the third day, firewood is piled onto a sand mandala in the northeast corner of the yard and is lit. The chanting of priests and playing of musical instruments continue for about two hours. The *mani rimdu* ceremony thus draws to a close.

The masked dance drama is an offering to various holy figures. Through their dancing, the priests protect, purify, and pray for good fortune and longevity on behalf of the multitudes.

The dance drama consists of these fourteen scenes: the Dance of the Golden Nectar; Messengers of the Guru Rinpoche; Defender of the Faith; Dance of the Drums; Masters of the Cemetery; Old Man; Guardians of the Dharma; Dance of the Zur-ra; Dance of the Dakini; the Yogi and the Novice; Dance of the Scavengers; Dance of the Swords; Dance of Spiritual Warfare; and Concluding Dance.

14 Defender of the Faith. This is a wrathful manifestation, one of the eight transformations of Padmasambhava. Wielding such Buddhist implements as the *vajra* (thunderbolt) in his right hand and the *purba* in his left, he crushes the evil spirit of the native Bon religion and converts the people to Buddhism.
15 Messengers of Guru Rinpoche. These are the tutelary spirits assigned to the four cardinal directions. Four holy figures—those in green mask and blue mask carrying small drums and those in red mask and yellow mask holding cymbals—dance around the altar. At the end, the four holy figures become one and attain enlightenment.
16 Masters of the Cemetery. The two Masters of the Cemetery, dressed as skeletons, are the helpers of Yama Rajah and pull around a "corpse," in which dwells an evil spirit. At the end, they hurl it to the ground. Two Tantric priests then join in, removing the evil spirit from the corpse and interring it. This demonstrates that, through the benevolence of Buddhism, even an evildoer can enter paradise after death.
17 The Old Man. Wearing Chinese-style garb, he gathers an audience around the stage and comically portrays the training and daily life activities that take place within the *gompa*.
18 & 19 Guardians of the Dharma. The eight holy guardians of the laws of Buddhism—the female spirit Lhamo, with her wrathful countenance (photo 18), Mahākala; the God of Warfare; Yamāntaka, who made Yama Rajah surrender; Kuvera (photo 19), Brahman; Ho; and Yama Rajah—dance around the altar and receive eight blessings from the Rinpoche for the triumph of good. The theme is that the goodness in Buddhism is superior to any evil.
20 Dance of the Dakini. Female spiritual figures, they are also the consorts and partners of Padmasambhava in Tantric training. The Dakini rescue the sufferer by flying to his or her aid. Five young male priests, dressed in their images, perform the dance.
21 Page 74. The summits of Everest and Lhotse glowing in the setting sun. In the evening the mountains worshiped by the villagers as gods entered their nighttime sleep.

8. Pangboche

Pangboche–Shomare–Orsho–Tsuro–Dingboche

2

Along the Everest Highway, Pangboche is the most interior of all the villages that boast year-round habitation. It is 3,901 meters (12,873 feet) above sea level. Pangboche consists of two villages: an upper village with a *gompa* at its center and a lower village with residences arrayed along a terraced hillside near the Imja Khola river. Together, the upper and lower villages have about fifty houses. Compared with Namche Bazar, the surface area of the arable land is small, and the houses themselves are small even though they have two stories. Daily life in this area seems restricted. I felt as if I caught a glimpse of the severe living conditions.

1 Page 75. Pangboche's upper village in January. Private residences stand as if snuggling together on the upper regions of the snow-covered terraced fields. The reddish brown *gompa* is also visible.
2 The lower village in August. In the stone-enclosed fields, wheat, potatoes, *kodo,* and other crops are planted. However, because of the small quantity of arable land, an abundant harvest in not expected.
3 A one-story private residence. Small houses such as this one are not usually found in other villages.
4 Young sisters standing in a doorway. The doors of Sherpa houses are all "push" doors. The kitchen is near the windows on the second floor.
5 A Sherpani washing her hair. The hair of Sherpa women grows long and remains uncut. They wash their hair about once a week, and it is quite a job.
6 A Sherpani combing her hair. After washing, the women linger in the sunshine, combing and drying their hair.
7 Playing marbles. In a garden filled with the summer's gentle sun, a group of girls play with the stones they found and brought back with them.
8 A *bhatti* kitchen. Responding to a guest's order, the young hostess begins to make tea.

9

Pangboche *gompa* is square-shaped and is two stories high like the *gompa* in other villages. In the front of the ground floor, the main holy figure is worshiped, and on both sides are located shelves for storing Buddhist scriptures. All over the left and right walls are richly colored paintings of various holy figures. At the front of the second floor, the major and various other holy figures are worshiped, but they are smaller than the ones on the first floor. In the wall paintings, "Guru Eight Transformations," the life story of Padmasambhava, the founder of Nyingma Buddhism and who is called Guru Rinpoche, the system of the Tantric universe, and other topics are dynamically rendered. Also, here, the scalp and hand bone from a yeti are allegedly preserved.

9 A priest, who usually stays at his own home, diligently pursues his Buddhist practices on the second floor of the *gompa*. It is said that this *gompa* has a three-hundred-year history, but there is no priest who permanently resides here. So when a visitor comes to visit the *gompa,* a priest who lives in his own house and is responsible for tending the monastery unlocks the door. While I was inspecting the *yeti* scalp, he began to chant.
10 Part of the front area of the second floor. From the ceiling hangs a drum called a *ghayu.* Among the various statues of holy figures behind it is a depiction of a sexual encounter between a man and a woman, called *yab yum.*
11 A wall on the second floor. The supreme Yoga, which is the very last Tantra, are said to be divided into three different classes: father (Guhyasamaja) Tantra; mother (Havajra) Tantra; and unique Tantra, the most complex of all supreme Yoga Tantras. The two holy figures in the picture are possibly members of the "mother" Tantra group.
12 The mandala of the supreme Yoga Tantra. On a second-floor wall, there are many paintings of a wrathful spirit holding his consort. The one here includes symbols of the Indian Shiva, such as a multitude of faces and arms, tiger undergarments, and a skull.

10

11

12

Following the highway deeper into the interior from Pangboche through Shomare *kharka,* we come to Orsho, where a household on the hillside runs a *bhatti.* Up until here, we have been walking along a valley road that skirts the banks of the Imja Khola, and so there has not been much of a view. But from here on, the hills open up. *Mani* stones are scattered here and there. The 8,516-meter-high (28,102-foot-high) Lhotse, which can be seen up ahead, becomes more formidable as we approach it. Leaving the main highway, which ascends to the left, along hills from Tsuro, we proceed straight ahead and cross a wooden bridge. Passing over the hills, we arrive at a valley where Dingboche starts to become visible. Dingboche, through which you must pass on the way to Chhukung, is famous for producing potatoes.

13 A *chorten* standing before Pangboche. In Pangboche, where an old *gompa* is located, there are many religious symbols, such as *chorten* and *mani* stones. The *chorten* in the picture protects the area from evil spirits.
14 The surprisingly well-constructed stone fences of Pangboche. Probably hundreds of years were spent piling up these stones. The mountains in the background are Ama Dablam (on the right), Lhotse (farther away), and Nuptse.
15 *Mani* stone and two Sherpani near Orsho. Even though this is a place far removed from habitation, Buddhist scriptures are carved on this great rock sitting on the side of the road. The scriptures are probably a prayer to the gods, entreating their protection for a journey into the interior. As is the custom, the descending Sherpani climbed down to the country village by passing along the left side of the *mani* stone.
16 Page 82. A summer *kharka* near Dingboche. Perhaps the villagers have gone down to Pangboche. No one was visible in the barn. Instead, the soft green fields of wheat, *kodo,* and potatoes welcomed me.

9. Chhukung

(Side Trip)
Chhukung

At 4,730 meters (15,609 feet) above sea level, Chhukung is the most interior *kharka* along the Imja Khola. The village of Pangboche has the right of common usage here. Over many years, the edges of the glaciers have retreated north, leaving behind places where grass could grow and the land could support human habitation. Up to Bibre, wheat and potatoes are planted in narrow stretches of arable land. But here, in Chhukung, there is no arable land at all. There are, however, two lodges. I stayed at one of them, but in the summer season, the villagers are busy taking care of cattle and milking the animals rather than catering to guests.

1 Page 83. Snow-covered Chhukung *kharka*. This *kharka* is located at the edge of a wide glacier. There was a significant snowfall, unusual for November, and the layout of the *kharka* was outlined in the snow.
2 Calves in the *kharka*. Calves born in the spring have come up to the *kharka* with their parents, which are herded away to the grass on the surrounding hillsides. Only the calves are left behind.
3 A Sherpani making potato bread. To make this bread, called *alu ko roti*, potatoes are ground up, a bit of wheat is added, and the ingredients are baked on an iron plate or flat stone. Potatoes were introduced to the Khumbu region in the middle of the eighteenth century. Since that time, they have become a major component of the Sherpa diet.
4 Children at a lodge.
5 Inside a *kharka* house. In the corner can be seen some cylindrical containers for making an unrefined rice brew called *chhang*. On the wall above the containers, a home shrine is installed. The structure of this house is like a miniaturized layout of a private house in a country village.
6 A lodge. This lodge is a one-story building that can accommodate ten people. On the left side of the entrance, there are wooden beds with mattresses.

7

After Kala Pattar and Gokyo Peak, Chhukung is one of the best scenic areas. Standing atop a hill rising up in the northern region of the *kharka,* we can see the view open up. To the east, a glacier zone, where the Lhotse Glacier meets the Imja Khola, spreads out. Beyond that is 8,463-meter-high (27,928-foot-high) Makalu. To the south, a 6,340-meter-high (20,922-foot-high) mountain, called Kang Leyamu—literally "Beautiful Snowy Peak"—by the villagers of Chhukung, shows off its shining Himalayan form. Looking to the south, we see the Rolwaling Mountains, including 6,957-meter-high (22,958-foot-high) Numbur, which the Sherpa of the Solu district worship as a holy mountain. Most impressive is a spectacular view of the great rock wall, differing in places by as much as 3,000 meters (9,900 feet) in height, that runs from 8,516-meter-high (28,102-foot-high) Lhotse, towering in the northern sky, to 7,855-meter-high (25,922-foot-high) Nuptse.

7 Pages 86 and 87. A distant view of Imja Glacier and Makalu. Many unnamed peaks surround Imja Glacier. On the right is Kang Leyamu (unnamed on the map), and to its left is a 7,000-meter-high (23,100-foot-high) mountain, also with an unnamed peak. Far in the distance, Makalu juts up.

8 Kang Leyamu and a mountaineering party. A mountaineering party moves on 6,160-meter-high (20,328-foot-high) Imja Tse (Island Peak), a mountain that one can climb with trekking permission. At the rear of the party is a Sherpani porter.

9 The south wall of Lhotse and Imja Tse (Island Peak) to the right. In late November, the jet stream brings wild storms, and the summit line from Lhotse to Nuptse is blurred with flurries of drifting snow. In the glacier zone, a sandstorm spiraled up, rumbling from the mountains could be heard, and soon a gust of wind advanced upon us.

10 The Rolwaling Mountains. In the southern sky, the peaks of the Rolwaling Mountains, including Numbur (at the far left), march into the distance.

10. From Pheriche to Everest Base Camp

Pheriche–Tukla–Lobuje–Gorakshep–Kala Pattar–Gorakshep–Everest Base Camp

1

At Pheriche, 4,252 meters (14,031 feet) above sea level, the symptoms of mountain sickness gradually begin to appear, and even parties of climbers stay over for two or three days to adjust to the altitude. There are many *kharka* between here and Gorakshep. The more popular the Everest climb has become, the more *bhatti* and lodges have been built, and they are open the year round. The right of common usage of these *kharka* is held by the village of Khumde. Like Tengboche and Pangboche, the name of this place has *che* at the end. According to a legend, a high-ranking priest named Che Rinpoche came to this area as a missionary.

1 Page 89. Looking down on Pheriche from the area between Tukla and Dingboche. Here, the Everest Highway extends through the middle of the *kharka* region, enclosed by stone fences on the mountains' flanks and the river region. The mountains seen in the background are 6,685-meter-high (22,060-foot-high) Kang Taiga (in the middle) and 6,623-meter-high (21,856-foot-high) Thamserku.
2 Winter mountain torrent. Surprisingly, this river, which collects snowmelt from the Khumbu Glacier and water from the Chola Khola, has no name. For the time being, I would like to name it "Khumbu Khola."
3 A *mani* stone standing outside the village of Pheriche, with 6,440-meter-high (21,252-foot-high) Cholotse ahead.
4 *Dzopkyo* on a snowy day. *Dzopkyo* are hybrids between yak and cattle. More precisely, *dzopkyo* refers to the male animal, and *dzom* to the female. Similarly, yak refers to the male, and *nak* to the female. Distinguishing between yak and *dzopkyo* is easy. A yak has a long, thick coat of hair, its body is large, and its horns protrude to the front. A *dzopkyo* is smaller, with thinner hair, and its horns point upward. Because *dzopkyo* do not realize that they can dig through the snow to reach the grass growing under it, they wander around in front of the barn when a heavy snowfall descends.

3

4

Tukla, located at the edge of the Khumbu Glacier, is 4,593 meters (15,157 feet) above sea level. Starting with this area, even small trees cannot grow. There are two lodges, but each is so small that it accommodates only ten guests. Because it is a day's trip from Pheriche to Lobuje, Tukla is usually a place that the trekker passes through, but it is an essential lunch-time stop for the Sherpa porters carrying the baggage.

The Sherpa follow a custom of "last child" inheritance. When the first and second son grow to adulthood, they leave home and become independent. But the last son takes care of the parents. Consequently, the parents often spoil their last son. The average number of children is about five.

5 Bearing the load to the Base Camp, at lower Tukla. For the most part, the loads belonging to climbing parties and trekkers are carried by Sherpa. However, of late, it has become difficult to find porters, so, quite often, *dzopkyo* are used.
6 Yaks grazing at Tukla *kharka*. In the summer, yaks can often be seen in the grasslands. The buildings in the background are lodges.
7 A lodge in Tukla. Because few people stay over here, the house is simple. Inside, the kitchen is to the right, and wooden beds are lined up on the left.
8 Gravestones memorializing the victims of accidents at upper Tukla. In the past, there were only seven such markers, but now there are over twenty. From Tukla to these memorials rises a notoriously sharp slope. Many people turn back at this point.
9 Yak and *dzopkyo* manure. The manure is collected, dried, and preserved as a major source of fuel.

6

7

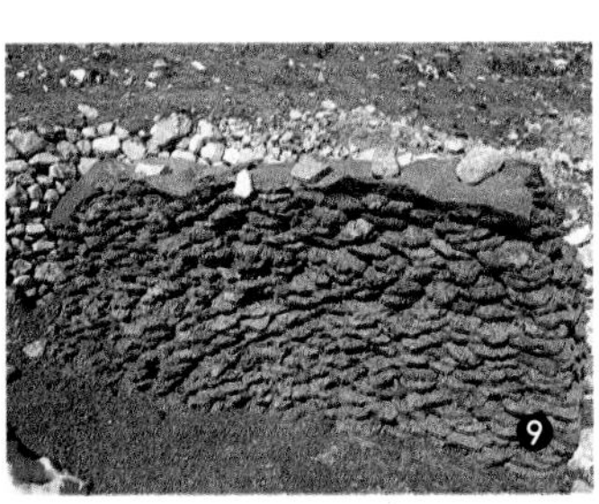
9

8

When people ascend to Lobuje, some 4,930 meters (16,269 feet) above sea level, they can feel the effects of the high elevation. Unless a trekker is experienced, altitude sickness can bring about such symptoms as vomiting and insomnia. Lobuje is the *kharka* area of Khumde. In the summer, it turns into a pasture, but in winter—the trekking season—the temperature drops to −40° C (−53° F). Even your breath freezes, and sleeping in a tent becomes difficult.

With 7,855-meter-high (25,922-foot-high) Nuptse looming ahead, four lodges stand quietly below the rocky mountains. These facilities are smaller than those at Namche Bazar, but they are bigger than those at Gorakshep, which is another half day farther into the interior. Thirty people can be accommodated at each lodge. Because more people might suffer from altitude sickness higher up at Gorakshep, they usually take a day trip to Kala Pattar or Base Camp from here.

10 Yaks for carrying loads, at upper Lobuje. When heavy snowfalls occur, all traces of human passage disappear. When this happens, yaks lead the way, stepping on the snow to pack it down, and the people follow in their wake.

11 A Sherpani knitting at the lodge. Most Sherpani knit when they have the time, making such personal items as socks, gloves, and caps. As soon as this Sherpani, who carried my load, arrived at the lodge in Lobuje, she started knitting in the light at the doorway. It was snowing outside, and her breath immediately condensed into a white haze.

12 Flowers blooming in a small *kharka* located in an ablation valley of the Khumbu Glacier. Because cattle do not eat this kind of grass, this place remains ungrazed.

Gorakshep is the last ***kharka*** on the Everest Highway. Probably because of its sandy ground, it gives the impression of being deserted. There are two small lodges. The name of the place means "Graveyard of Crows." Climbing from here to Kala Pattar, to the north, takes about an hour and a half. Gorakshep is the best vista point of the whole course, where the high peaks of the Khumbu Mountains, including the 8,848-meter-high (29,028-foot-high) Everest, can be seen.

Going from Gorakshep to the Base Camp, which is 5,300 meters (17,490 feet) above sea level, takes a climb of about four hours, stepping through the glacier's icy snow and occasionally passing ice pillars and crevasses. At the end of the Khumbu Glacier is a world of icy snow and rock chips. For the Sherpa who live in the foothills of these towering mountains, the mountains themselves are gods, whose providence bestows rain and cash income.

13 The 7,855-meter-high (25,922-foot-high) Nuptse as viewed from Lobuje. From here 6,501-meter-high (21,453-foot-high) Taweche and 6,440-meter-high (21,252-foot-high) Cholotse can be seen.
14 The 7,161-meter-high (23,631-foot-high) Pumo Ri as viewed from Gorakshep. Pumo Ri means "Bride's Peak."
15 Khumbu Glacier as viewed from halfway up Kala Pattar. The mountains to the rear are 5,820-meter-high (19,206-foot-high) Kongma Tse (Melhra), 5,806-meter-high (19,160-foot-high) Pokalde, and others to the left of Khumbu Glacier.
16 Everest Base Camp, built on the icy snow 5,300 meters (17,490 feet) above sea level. Tents have been set up for a group of mountain climbers who are aiming for the summit of the mountain.
17 Ice towers and 6,640-meter-high (21,912-foot-high) Khumbutse.
18 Pages 98 and 99. Mount Everest and Nuptse as viewed from Kala Pattar. The top of Kala Pattar has a space that only two people can stand on. Everest is Sagarmatha in Nepali. *Sagar* means "big sky" or "world," and *matha* means "head" or "peak." So, taken together the name means "Peak of the World."
19 Page 100. Western Cum as viewed from the Base Camp. Many climbing groups traverse this glacier, aiming for the peak from South Col.

17

18

11. Exotic Mountain Flowers

Expert Opinion by Hiroo Kanai (The National Science Museum)
The Himalayas are a treasure trove of high mountain plant life. The flowers recorded here are only those seen during my trekking in the area beyond Namche Bazar. However, because summer, when the flowers are blooming, is also the rainy season, mountain vistas cannot be expected.

Meconopsis horridula (poppy family)
Upper Lobuje area

Corydalis cashmeriana (poppy family)
Lobuje area

Arenaria (pink family)
Near Sanarsa

Geranium donianum
(geranium family) Near Gokyo

The family names of these flowers are given in parentheses. If the specific name is not known, then only generic names are listed.

Thalictrum reniforme
(buttercup family) Near Sanarsa

Delphinium drepanocentrum
(buttercup family) Near Sanarsa

Ranunculus (buttercup family)
Tukla

Rosa macrophylla (rose family)
Near Sanarsa

Parnassia nubicola (saxifrage family)
Near Panka

Potentilla eriocarpa (rose family)
Gokyo

Saxifraga brachypoda
(saxifrage family) Gokyo

Saxifraga brunonis (saxifrage family)
Lower Lobuje area

Saxifraga mucronulata
(saxifrage family) Lobuje

Rhodiola himalensis (orpine family)
Upper Lobuje area

Anaphalis nepalensis
(composite family) Dole

Anaphalis triplinervis
(composite family) Near Gokyo

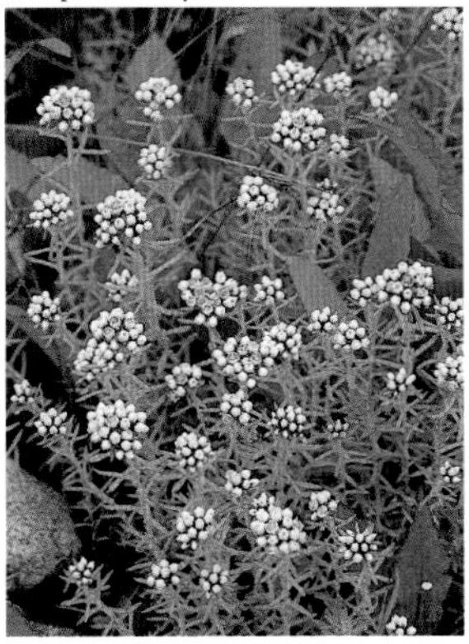

Anaphalis contorta (composite family)
Near Sanarsa

Anaphalis, (composite family)
Lobuje

Anaphalis (composite family)
Upper Lobuje area

Anaphalis (composite family)
Near Sanarsa

Anaphalis (composite family)
Upper Lobuje area

Leontopodium jacotianum
(composite family) Namche Bazar

Leontopodium monocephalum
(composite family) Chhukung

Tanacetum gossypinum
(composite family) Upper Lobuje area

Saussurea simpsoniana
(composite family) Upper Lobuje area

Saussurea gossypiphora
(composite family) Changri Glacier

Saussurea gossypiphora
(composite family) Gokyo

Saussurea nepalensis
(composite family) Upper Lobuje area

Erigeron (composite family)
Gokyo

Aster himalaicus (composite family)
Near Luza

Aster albescens (composite family)
Near Sanarsa

Waldheimia glabra (composite family)
Changri Glacier

Inula royleana (composite family)
Near Namche Bazar

Rhododendron campanulatum
(heath family) Tengboche

Cremanthodium nepalense
(composite family) Gokyo

Nannoglottis hookeri
(composite family) Near Dole

Codonopsis thalictrifolia
(bellflower family) Near Panka

Cyananthus incanus
(bellflower family) Gokyo

Campanula (bellflower family)
Sanarsa

Rhododendron lepidotum
(heath family) Near Sanarsa

Androsace mucronifolia
(primrose family) Lower Lobuje area

Primula wollastonii
(primrose family) Near Sanarsa

Primula sikkimensis
(primrose family) Lobuje

Gentiana depressa (gentian family)
Below the Thame Gompa

Gentiana algida
(gentian family) Lobuje

Swertia multicaulis
(gentian family) Upper Lobuje area

Swertia multicaulis
(gentian family) Lobuje

Pedicularis roylei (figwort family)
Upper Lobuje area

Pedicularis siphonantha
(figwort family) Gokyo

Pedicularis trichoglossa
(figwort family) Lobuje

Pedicularis longiflora (figwort family)
Gokyo

Pedicularis scullyana
(figwort family) Lower Lobuje area

Oreosolen wattii (figwort family)
Lobuje

Trigonotis rotundifolia
(borage family) Gokyo

Glechoma (mint family)
Gokyo

Polygonum affinis (polygonum family)
Lower Gokyo area

Salvia (mint family)
Namche Bazar

Phlomis rotata (mint family)
Lower Gokyo area

Bistorta millettii (polygonum family)
Lobuje

Bistorta vaccinifolia
(polygonum family) Chhukung

Lillium nepalense (lily family)
Near Namche Bazar

Ponerorchis chusua (orchid family)
Near Sanarsa

Notholirion macrophyllum
(lily family) Near Sanarsa

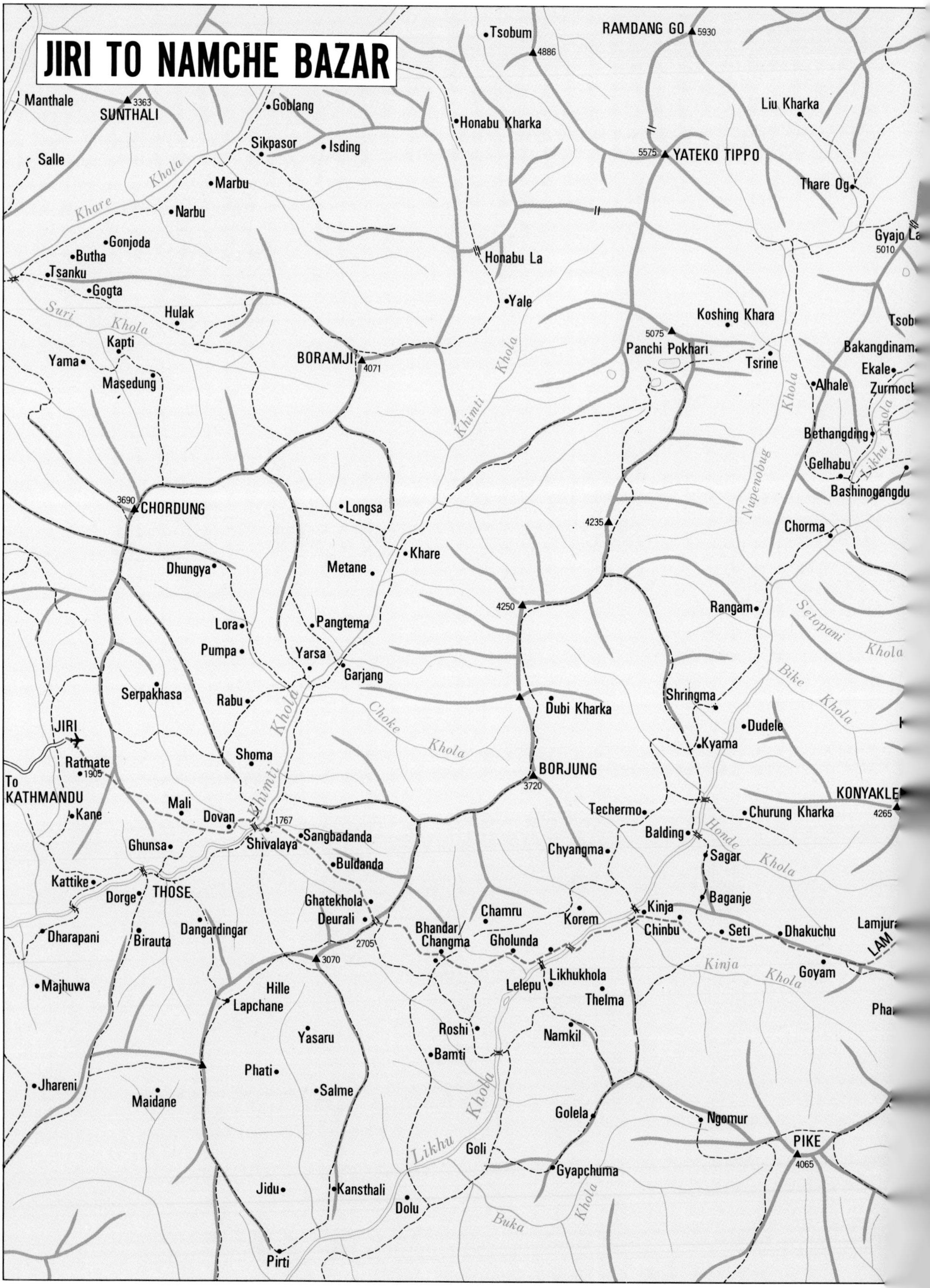
JIRI TO NAMCHE BAZAR
Tsobum
RAMDANG GO
5930
4886
Manthale
3363
SUNTHALI
Goblang
Honabu Kharka
Liu Kharka
Sikpasor
Isding
Salle
5575
YATEKO TIPPO
Khare Khola
Marbu
Thare Og
Narbu
Gyajo La
5010
Gonjoda
Butha
Honabu La
Tsanku
Gogta
Yale
Suri Khola
Hulak
Koshing Khara
5075
Kapti
Panchi Pokhari
Yama
BORAMJI
4071
Tsrine
Bakangdinam
Ekale
Masedung
Khimti Khola
Alhale
Zurmoc
Nupenobug Khola
Likhu Khola
Bethangding
Gelhabu
Bashinogangdu
3690
CHORDUNG
Longsa
4235
Chorma
Khare
Dhungya
Metane
4250
Rangam
Setopani Khola
Lora
Pangtema
Pumpa
Yarsa
Garjang
Serpakhasa
Rabu
Dubi Kharka
Shringma
Bike Khola
Choke Khola
Dudele
JIRI
Kyama
Ratmate
1905
Shoma
BORJUNG
To KATHMANDU
3720
KONYAKLE
Mali
Dovan
Khimti Khola
Techermo
Churung Kharka
4265
Kane
1767
Balding
Honde Khola
Ghunsa
Shivalaya
Sangbadanda
Chyangma
Sagar
Buldanda
Kattike
Dorge
THOSE
Baganje
Ghatekhola
Chamru
Korem
Kinja
Deurali
Bhandar/Changma
Chinbu
Seti
Dhakuchu
Lamjura
Dharapani
Birauta
Dangardingar
2705
Gholunda
LAM
3070
Kinja Khola
Goyam
Likhukhola
Lelepu
Hille
Thelma
Majhuwa
Lapchane
Pha
Roshi
Yasaru
Namkil
Bamti
Jhareni
Phati
Salme
Maidane
Golela
Ngomur
Likhu Khola
PIKE
Goli
4065
Gyapchuma
Jidu
Kansthali
Dolu
Buka Khola
Pirti

Trashingo
Tengboche
Khumjung
Khumde
Sanarsa
Thamo
Tesho
Pare
Phurte
Hotel Everest View
Syangboche
NAMCHE BAZAR
Thame Khola
Bhote Kosi
Dudh Kosi
PIGPHERA GO SHAR
6730
PANAYO TOPPA
6696
TENG KANGPOCHE
6500
6666
PIGPHERA GO NUP
KWANGDE
6011
Jorsale
Monjo
Kyashar Khola
Benkar
Chumoa
4431
Zurmoche Gl.
Lumding Gl.
KHATANG
6853
NUMBUR
6957
Lumding Kharka
Lumding La
Gyajo
Samga
Phakding
2652
Tsermang
Nyasung Dingma
KARYOLAUG
6681
More La
KUSUM KANGURU
6367
Ghat
Chumlo
Kusum Khola
Kyomma
Chapling
Chaumrikharka
5813
5313
Dankilobug
Dudhkunde Gl.
Lumding Khola
LUKLA
Thadarbug
Rambug
Surkhe
Suruke Khola
Charamko
Luza Khola
Basa Khola
Chutok La
Phuiyan
Rowuche Khola
Phuiyan Khola
Khari La
3081
Dudh Kosi
Beni Khola
4511
Kharte
Phungmuche
Deku Khola
Pangkarma
Deku
Siteling
Agang
Kharikhola
Nyungso
Mapung
Ringmo
Jubing
Gongu Kharka
Thupten Chhulin
Tragsindho La
3071
Phuleli
Manidingma
Chhi
Jule
Pangkongma
Junbesi
Tragsindho
Khamche
Solung
Lelung
Domfug
Junbesi Khola
Nashing
Chhanga
Amdung Kharka
Hinku Khola
Salbesi
Beni Khola
Andheri
Phera
Thulp Dhunga
DANDA
Solu Khola
Ledingma
Simle
Wapsa Khani
N
PHAPLU
Basha
0
5
10km

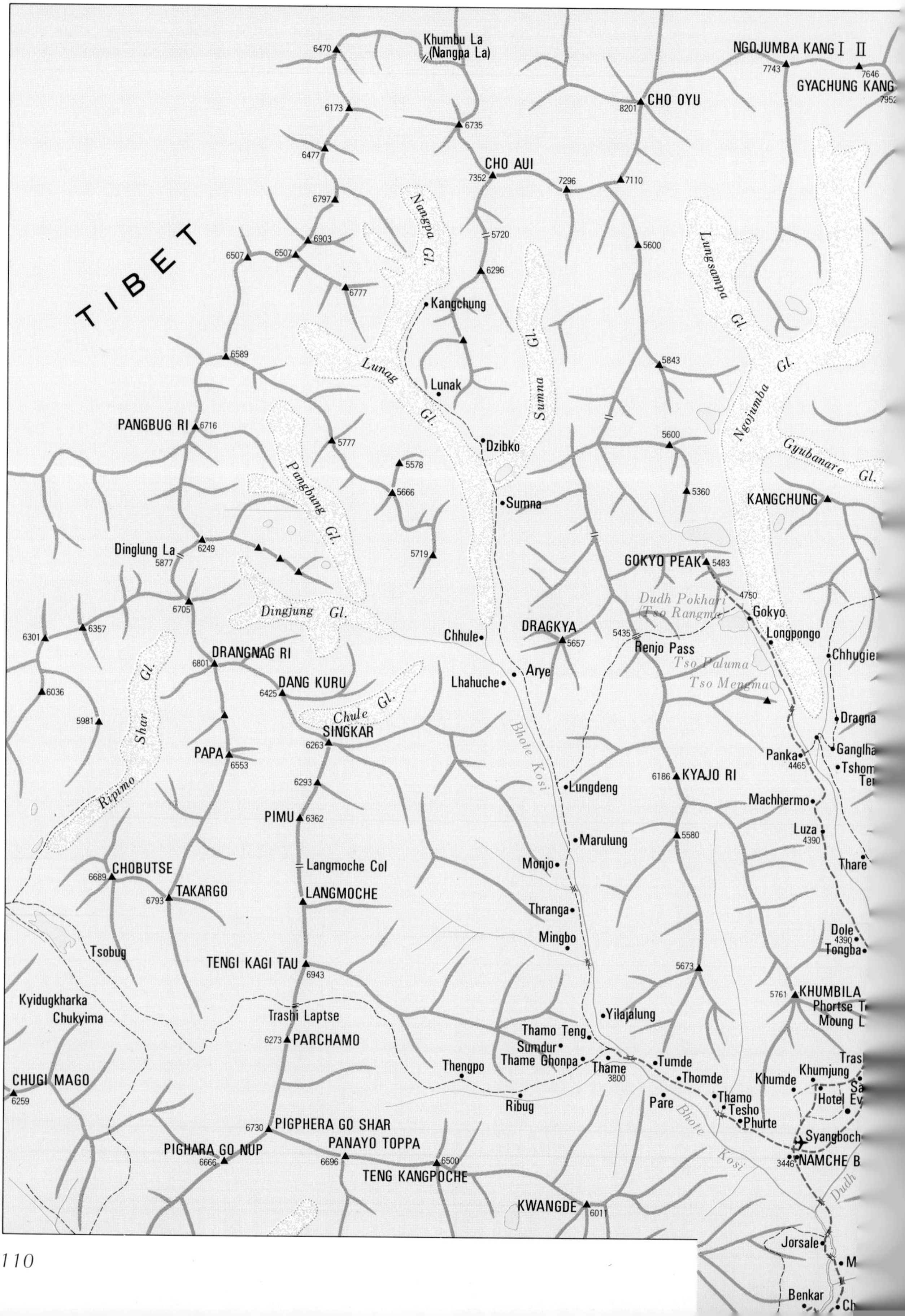
TIBET
Khumbu La
(Nangpa La)
6470
6173
6735
6477
CHO AUI
7352
7296
7110
NGOJUMBA KANG I II
7743
7646
GYACHUNG KANG
CHO OYU
8201
6797
Nangpa Gl.
5720
6903
6507
6507
6777
6296
Kangchung
Sumna Gl.
5600
Lungsampa Gl.
6589
Lunag Gl.
Lunak
5843
Ngojumba Gl.
PANGBUG RI
6716
5777
Dzibko
5600
Gyubanare Gl.
5578
Pangbung Gl.
5666
Sumna
5360
KANGCHUNG
Dinglung La
5877
6249
5719
GOKYO PEAK
5483
6705
Dingjung Gl.
Dudh Pokhari
(Tso Rangma)
4750
Gokyo
6301
6357
Chhule
DRAGKYA
5657
5435
Renjo Pass
Longpongo
DRANGNAG RI
6801
Tso Paluma
Chhugie
Shar Gl.
6036
DANG KURU
6425
Lhahuche
Arye
Tso Mengma
Chule Gl.
5981
SINGKAR
6263
Dragna
Bhote Kosi
Panka
4465
Ganglha
PAPA
6553
Tshom
Ripimo
6293
Lungdeng
6186
KYAJO RI
Machhermo
PIMU
6362
Luza
4390
Marulung
5580
Langmoche Col
Monjo
Thare
CHOBUTSE
6689
TAKARGO
6793
LANGMOCHE
Thranga
Mingbo
Dole
4390
Tongba
Tsobug
TENGI KAGI TAU
6943
5673
Kyidugkharka
Chukyima
Trashi Laptse
Yilajalung
5761
KHUMBILA
Phortse
Moung
PARCHAMO
6273
Thamo Teng
Sumdur
Thame Ghonpa
Thame
3800
Tumde
Thomde
Thengpo
Trashi
Khumde
Khumjung
Hotel Ev
CHUGI MAGO
6259
Ribug
Pare
Thamo
Tesho
Phurte
Bhote Kosi
PIGPHERA GO SHAR
6730
Syangboche
PIGHARA GO NUP
6666
PANAYO TOPPA
6696
6500
3446
NAMCHE B
TENG KANGPOCHE
Dudh
KWANGDE
6011
Jorsale
Benkar

NAMCHE BAZAR TO EVEREST B.C.

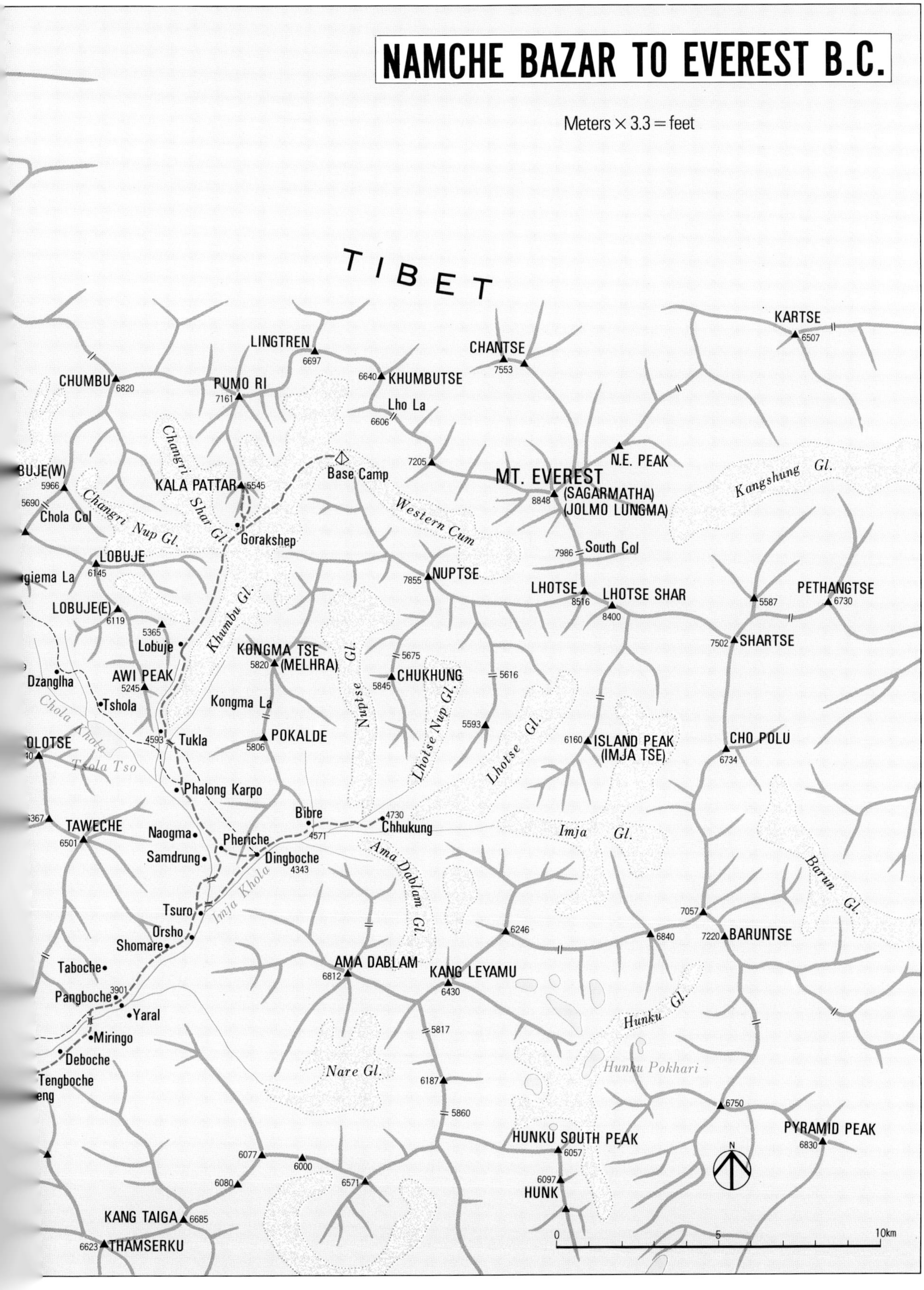

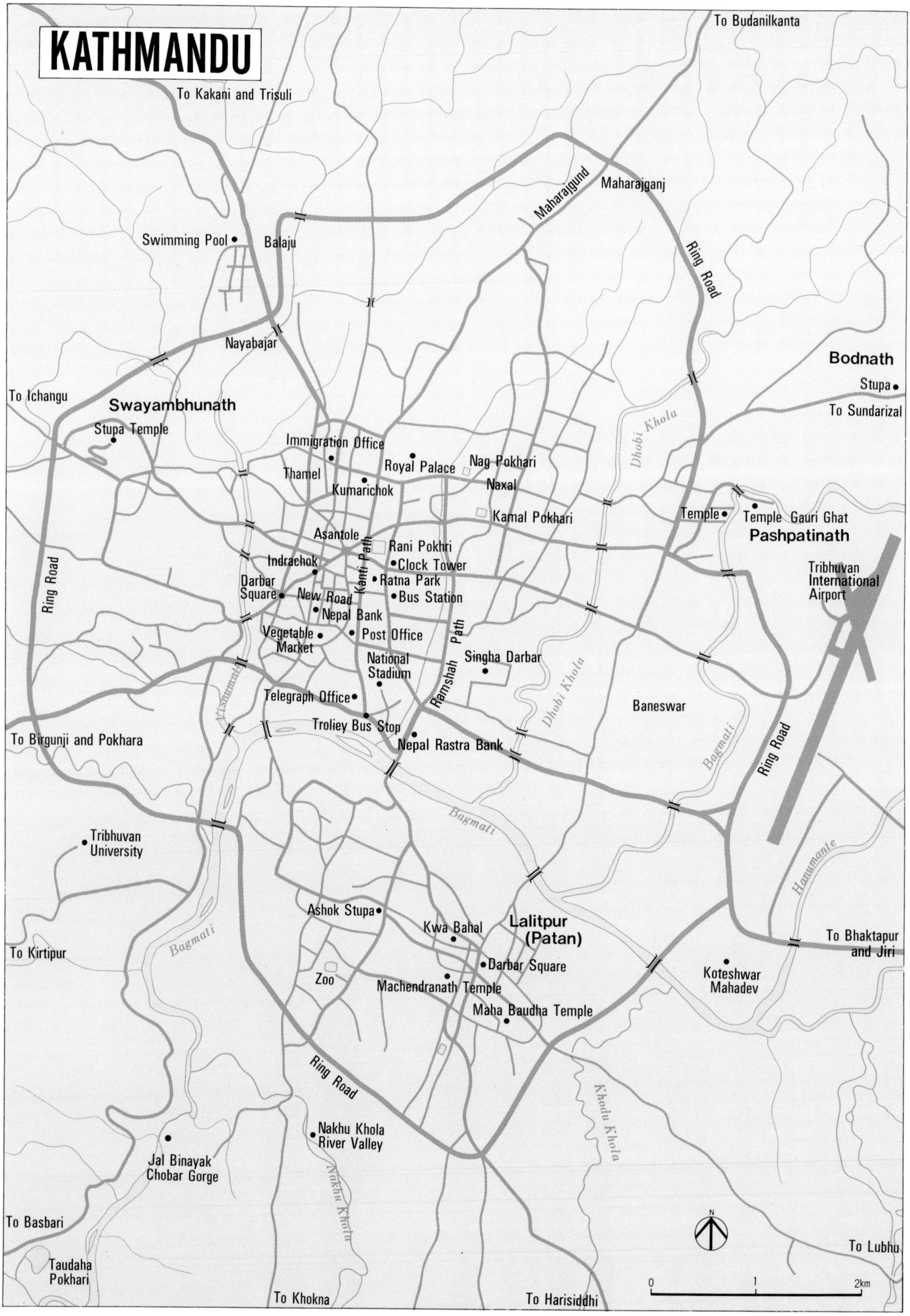
KATHMANDU
To Kakani and Trisuli
To Budanilkanta
Maharajgunj
Maharajganj
Ring Road
Swimming Pool
Balaju
Nayabajar
Bodnath
Stupa
To Sundarizal
To Ichangu
Swayambhunath
Stupa Temple
Immigration Office
Royal Palace
Nag Pokhari
Thamel
Kumarichok
Naxal
Dhobi Khola
Kamal Pokhari
Temple
Temple Gauri Ghat
Pashpatinath
Asantole
Rani Pokhri
Indrachok
Clock Tower
Kanti Path
Tribhuvan International Airport
Ring Road
Darbar Square
New Road
Ratna Park
Bus Station
Nepal Bank
Vegetable Market
Post Office
Ramshah Path
National Stadium
Singha Darbar
Telegraph Office
Baneswar
Bishnumati
Dhobi Khola
Trolley Bus Stop
Nepal Rastra Bank
To Birgunji and Pokhara
Bagmati
Ring Road
Bagmati
Tribhuvan University
Hanumante
Ashok Stupa
Kwa Bahal
Lalitpur (Patan)
To Bhaktapur and Jiri
To Kirtipur
Bagmati
Darbar Square
Koteshwar Mahadev
Zoo
Machendranath Temple
Maha Baudha Temple
Ring Road
Khodu Khola
Nakhu Khola River Valley
Jal Binayak Chobar Gorge
Nakhu Khola
To Basbari
N
To Lubhu
Taudaha Pokhari
0
1
2km
To Khokna
To Harisiddhi

Getting the Most Out of Trekking

What You Should Know Before Trekking

The Everest Highway

The name Everest Highway is not an official one, for there is no thoroughfare fit to be called a highway. Although trekkers follow the roads used by local people, they become, along the way, rugged mountain trails, and at the end of the Highway, you are walking on glaciers.

If travelers take the bus from Kathmandu, the starting point for the trek is Jiri. From there to the Everest Base Camp takes about twelve days on foot. If they travel by plane, then the trek starts from Lukla and takes about six days.

The appeal of the Everest Highway lies, first, in an intimate view of the towering Himalayan peaks, including the world's highest, 8,848-meter-high (29,028-foot-high) Mount Everest, and second, in the chance to visit the towns of the Sherpa and get a feel for the life of these highland Tibetan Buddhists. The Sherpa live in two areas: Solu, which is the lower of the two, and Khumbu, the higher.

The Solu area starts at Shivalaya, some three hours' walk from Jiri. White-walled, two-story, stone houses, characteristic of the Sherpa, start to appear. In the low-lying river area, however, the Indo-Aryan Brahman and Chhetri peoples and the Rai and Tamang peoples live together.

The itinerary for trekking the Solu area involves crossing almost straight from west to east, with high peaks rising to the north, and ridges and marshes, both large and small, spreading across the south.

Entering the Dudh Kosi basin, you proceed north along the river. After traversing the 3,081-meter-high (10,167-foot-high) Khari La, you arrive at the Khumbu area. From Lukla, you proceed to the Sherpa town of Namche Bazar. From there, going through Tengboche and Pangboche, you arrive at Everest Base Camp.

As for the views of the mountains, first, in the Solu area, you see 6,957-meter-high (22,958-foot-high) Numbur, which the Sherpa revere as a holy mountain. From Tragsindho La, Mera Peak can be seen on the left bank of the Dudh Kosi. From Tengboche, 6,812-meter-high (21,480-foot-high) Ama Dablam looms close by. From 5,545-meter-high (18,298-foot-high) Kala Pattar, you have an expansive view of Mount Everest, and of Lhotse, and Pumo Ri, all of which are over 7,000 meters.

On the Thame side trip, you can see the Rolwaling Mountains. The view from Gokyo Peak is as good as that from Kala Pattar. Nearby, you can look up at such vast mountains as Cho Oyu and Gyachung Kang. From Chhukung, the south wall of Lhotse and Kang Leyamu can be seen.

The mountains of the Khumbu area form a group, though they still possess the characteristics of independent peaks. Even though the Himalaya Mountains are extensive, there is no superior place from which to see the mountain spectacle.

Obtaining a Trekking Permit

In order to go trekking, a permit, issued by the government of Nepal, is required. In the large villages along the route, there are checkpoints where you have to show your permit. If you do not have a permit, you will immediately be turned back to Kathmandu.

Anyone can get a permit or, for a fee, can arrange for a travel agent to do so on his or her behalf. Two photographs (5 centimeters by 5 centimeters or 2 inches by 2 inches) and a 1-rupee revenue stamp are required. There is also a fee of 90 rupees per week. Also required is written proof that you have exchanged money in the amount of about US $5 for each day of your stay. This certificate is issued by banks and regular hotels. Areas for trekking courses are limited, and the route presented in this book is within the permissible range. From Thame, you are not permitted to pass over Trashi Laptsa or to enter the interior regions around Bhote Kosi.

Currency Exchange

The local currency is the Nepali rupee, which is divided into 100 paises. Money can be exchanged at the Kathmandu airport, the Nepal Rastra Bank located within the city, or any first-class hotel. At the time of the exchange, you should acquire a money exchange certificate. Failing to do so may cause trouble later. Once your money is converted into Nepali rupees, only ten percent of that currency can be exchanged again into the currency of your own country. You should estimate your budget carefully and avoid exchanging more money than what you need. As of 1990, $1 is 28.4 rupees.

Rupee paper money is available in 1,000, 500, 100, 50, 20, 10, 5, 2, and 1 rupee units. Coins are for 1 rupee, 50, 25, 10, 5, 2, and 1 paises. In practice, however, coins below 5 paises are not used. Since the money is not marked in arabic numbers, it can be quite confusing if you are unfamiliar with it. During a trek, it is more convenient to have small bills, such as 10 rupees or less, for purchasing *cheea* (milk tea) or something at a *bhatti,* lodge, or other resting spot.

Guides and Porters

Sherpa (guides) and porters, both of whom are essential for trekking, should usually be reserved through travel agencies in Kathmandu. In order to save time, however, it is convenient to make a reservation through your domestic travel agent.

The standard fee for a Sherpa is about 100 rupees per day, with the employer, or *saheb,* paying for the guide's meals. A porter costs about 80 rupees per day and takes care of his or her own meals. Trekkers can travel without a Sherpa or porters, but it is often inconvenient and it is easy for a lone trekker to be misunderstood. I cannot, therefore, recommend traveling alone unless a trekker is very experienced.

The role of the Sherpa is to take care of everything involved in the trekking: leading the way, setting up and taking down the tent at the camping site, hiring and dismissing porters, providing meals, and so on. At the beginning of a trek, it is essential to discuss in detail your desires, from the entire itinerary of the trip to each day's particular schedule. Even the schedule for daily morning tea and each meal need to be set forth clearly. Once these matters are settled, most arrangements proceed as desired, even though everything is left to the Sherpa. A capable Sherpa will immediately understand the *saheb's* intention.

Additional fees are about 80 rupees a day for a cook and about 60 rupees per day for a kitchen helper. Both of them prepare meals.

Accommodations

Most locations for staying overnight and for camping along the way are predetermined. The Sherpa sets up a tent at a suitable place. If you want the tent in a particular location, you have to inform the Sherpa. Sherpas will do their best to please you. Rather than feeling dissatisfied, it is much kinder to convey your preferences from the very beginning. However, you have to choose one leader in the party to whom you will address your instructions.

Trekkers should limit the things they carry to valuables, cameras, and rain gear, because climbing in high elevations can cause ten pounds of baggage to feel like thirty. Ordinarily, a porter can carry luggage weighing sixty-five pounds. Sherpa carry only their own equipment.

In winter, for accommodations at 4,000 meters (13,200 feet) or higher, a tent is unsuitable, and trekkers should stay at a lodge or *bhatti.*

Food

Menus during trekking are generally fixed. First, morning tea is brought to the tent. For breakfast, there are toast or *capati* (thin, baked cakes) with an egg dish, jam and butter, instant coffee or milk tea. Lunch consists of rice or *capati,* potatoes, curried vegetables with sausage, fried noodles, a macaroni dish, and tea. Dinner includes broth or pottage, rice and chicken or buffalo, curried potatoes, canned fish, *dal* beans cooked as a soup, fresh vegetable salads with onions and tomatoes, and canned pineapple or fruit cocktail for dessert. Coffee and tea are also served.

Provisions can be purchased in Kathmandu. If someone is trekking alone, it would be advisable to discuss with the Sherpa the items and amounts to be purchased according to the length of the trip and the choice of menu. Because the Sherpa eat twice as much as the *saheb,* provisions will be inadequate unless an additional quantity is purchased.

During the trek, menus are designed to change every day, but the more days that pass and the higher you climb, the more you grow tired of the extensive menus. It is easier to eat steamed potatoes and other simple foods. If possible, you should bring snacks from home, such as biscuits, chocolates, and sweets. Cooking with oil is common, but because local oil may cause diarrhea, you may want to bring your own vegetable oil.

Local foods eaten by the porters include *dyuro,* a kind of boiled dumpling made from buckwheat flour, and *kodo* (millet) eaten with a dip. A bread called *alu ko roti,* made from ground potatoes and flour and baked on a flat stone or iron griddle, is eaten with *khorasani,* a mixture of garlic, salt, and hot peppers, with a seasoning called *maltse,* or with cheese spread over it. A raw, unrefined liquor called *chhang* is available. The best kind is made from rice. The fresh liquid floating on the top of this beverage, called *ningu,* is similar in taste to Japanese sake. Distilled *chhang* is called *roksi* and is equivalent to 25-proof spirits. All these drinks are available at the *bhatti* along the Highway, but at high altitudes a person feels the effects of alcohol very quickly, so it is better to consume liquor in small amounts.

Clothing and Equipment

Clothing should include everything from shorts and short-sleeved shirts to down garments so that you can trek in the subtropical zones at elevations of under

1,000 meters (3,300 feet), the temperate zones that rise to 3,000 meters (9,900 feet), and beyond that to the frigid zones at 4,000 meters (13,200 feet) and above. In addition, at all times except winter, when you stay at a lodge, a *bhatti,* or especially at a private house in the Namche Bazar area or in a village lower in elevation, you should be aware that you will be plagued by fleas. Bedbugs and ticks are also plentiful, and in the lower areas particularly, mosquitos are a problem, so it is necessary to carry insect repellent. Consequently, except for rainy days, it is more comfortable to stay in a tent. Since there are also times when you will be unable to stay at a lodge, *bhatti,* or the like, you are well advised to bring your own tent. Some items can be purchased or rented in Kathmandu; consult the list on the previous page.

Climate

The seasons of the Himalaya Mountains can be divided into two: a dry winter season from December to February, and a rainy summer season from June to September. In winter, the air flow in the upper atmosphere is westerly; and in the summer, easterly. The changes that bring the different seasons occur from the north-south movement of the jet stream through the upper atmosphere. The movement and its timing are relatively straightforward. In the summer monsoon season, rain falls intermittently all day. The period between March and May, just prior to the rains, is called the premonsoon season. October and November, following the monsoons, is called the postmonsoon season. These pre- and post-monsoon seasons, when good weather is consistent because of the weakening of the upper atmospheric jet stream, are favorable periods for trekking.

The best time for trekking is during the thirty days from mid-October to mid-November, during the post-monsoon season. The autumn days are refreshing and sunny, and the mountains can be seen clearly. By the latter half of November, one morning, without warning, gusting winds begin to blow and the dust swirls. Strong winds that make walking difficult may continue for four or five days. This signals the coming of the winter jet stream.

The next best time for trekking is March and April, during the premonsoon season. Day after day, the sunlight brightens, and the temperature rises. You can proceed with your day's plans without worrying about when the sun goes down.

The third best time is during the winter. After the beginning of January, the weather tends to be highly stable. In some years 1 to 2 meters (up to 6½ feet) of snow fall in winter. Throughout my more than ten years of trekking, I have noticed that the heavy snowfalls are concentrated mostly from December 25 to 30, and that there have been no large snowfalls in January. Winter

Trekking Checklist

	under 3,000 meters (9,900 feet)		3,000–5,000 meters (9,900 feet)		Purchase or rent in Kathmandu
Item	Spring & Fall	Winter	Spring & Fall	Winter	
Tent with rain fly	•	•	•	•	•
Small bag	•	•	•	•	
Sleeping bag	•	•	•	•	
Down-filled clothing			•	•	
Down-filled pants			•	•	
Anorak with wind jacket & trousers				•	
Mountain boots			•	•	
Walking shoes	•	•	•	•	
Lightweight climbing boots	•	•	•	•	
Sunglasses	•	•	•	•	
Mattress	•	•	•	•	•
Thermos	•	•	•	•	
Canteen	•		•		
Headlamp	•	•	•	•	
Long spats			•	•	
Picks				•	•
Eisen				•	
Jacket		•	•	•	
Sweater		•	•	•	
Shirt	•	•	•	•	
Short-sleeved shirt	•				•
Short pants	•				•
Woolen underwear			•	•	
Cotton underwear	•		•		
Woolen cap			•	•	
Sun hat	•	•	•		
Woolen gloves			•	•	•
Cotton gloves	•		•		
Socks	•	•	•	•	
Mountain-climbing pants		•	•	•	
Towel	•	•	•	•	•
Scarf			•	•	
Folding umbrella	•	•	•	•	
Knife	•	•	•	•	•
Rubber sandals	•	•	•		•
Medical supplies	•	•	•	•	
Facial soap	•	•	•	•	•
Toothbrush	•	•	•	•	
Toothpaste	•	•	•	•	
Sewing equipment	•	•	•	•	
Lighter	•	•	•	•	
Matches	•	•	•	•	•
Notebook	•	•	•	•	•
Writing instruments	•	•	•	•	
Maps	•	•	•	•	•
Compass	•	•	•	•	
Toilet paper	•	•	•	•	•
Oil cooking stove	•	•	•	•	•
Candles	•	•	•	•	•
Plastic fuel bottles	•	•	•	•	
Plastic water bottles (5 liters / 10½ pints)	•	•	•	•	•
Pot	•	•	•	•	•
Pan	•	•	•	•	•
Turner	•	•	•	•	•
Kettle	•	•	•	•	•
Kitchen knife	•	•	•	•	•
Spatula	•	•	•	•	•
Ladle	•	•	•	•	•
Cup	•	•	•	•	•
Eating utensils	•	•	•	•	•
Cleanser	•	•	•	•	•
Pot cleaner	•	•	•	•	•
Insect repellent	•		•		•

often brings strong winds, however, so when climbing at elevations of 4,000 meters (13,200 feet) or above in the Khumbu Range, it is too cold to remove your down clothing even on a sunny day. For winter trekking, be sure to take precautions against the cold.

Trekking during the July-August monsoon season yields little in mountain viewing. Nevertheless, once in a while, a mountain profile can be seen during the brief moments of sunlight between rainstorms. More so than in other seasons, the intermittent sun illuminating the glistening snow of the mountaintops gives them a transcendental appearance. Monsoon season also brings the many beautiful flowers that decorate the earth.

Temperature changes over the course of a day are severe. A difference of 20° C (68° F), or more, can exist between daytime and morning or evening. The disparity is especially dramatic during the postmonsoon season. Before sunrise and after sunset, the temperature drops sharply. As the morning warms the air, the temperature rises quickly to around 30° C (85° F). You therefore need to rotate your clothing, from down garments to T-shirts.

High-Altitude Sickness

When a trekker ascends to a high altitude, the lack of oxygen, in particular, can bring about a variety of physical reactions. The actual cause of high-altitude sickness is unknown, but other factors that may exacerbate it are cold temperatures, dry air, and ultraviolet radiation. There are varying degrees to which the illness attacks, and even a healthy person may manifest such symptoms as listlessness, headaches, shortness of breath, nausea, loss of appetite, insomnia, coughing, and edema. If someone is already ill, climbing to a high elevation will worsen his or her condition. The high-altitude sickness prevents someone from concentrating, exercising good judgement, or thinking clearly. If the climber deals with the environment intelligently, altitudes of up to 4,000 or 5,000 meters (13,000 to 16,000 feet) do not present a danger. If not, the climber may face serious illness or death.

Slight symptoms of high-altitude sickness can start at about 3,000 meters (9,900 feet). Beginning at around 4,000 meters (13,000 feet), the symptoms can become quite pronounced. As the symptoms worsen, a person can experience difficulty breathing and sleeping during rest stops or at night, rather than during daytime activities. A climber may begin having headaches in the morning and may find that just getting up is quite a chore. Because the face puffs up and the hands and feet swell, the symptoms are identifiable to oneself and others.

In spite of these warnings, the trekker can employ a variety of countermeasures. You should pace yourself and take care not to climb, all at once, heights that differ by 500 or more meters (1,650 or more feet). You should also drink sufficient liquids during and between meals to prevent dehydration. The required daily intake of liquid is 3 to 4 liters (6¼ to 8½ pints). As much as possible, breath only through your nose so that your throat is protected and your mouth does not get too dry. If a headache starts about an hour after arriving at your destination, rather than lying down, you should dress warmly and take a light walk, which increases your body's energy level and helps you to recover more quickly. These precautions are essential for trekking along the Everest Highway.

The discomfort induced by high-altitude sickness can only be understood by someone who has experienced it. The remedy is found in simply inhaling more oxygen, though this is only a temporary relief, or descending in altitude by about 1,000 meters (3,300 feet). If you want to be prudent, you should immediately climb down the mountain on the back of a *dzopkyo* or yak.

Ethnic Diversity

With its variety of tribal groups, Nepal is rightly called a melting pot. This multitude can be divided into two main families, the Indo-Aryan and the Mongoloid. Most of the people live on agricultural products such as rice, barley, corn, *kodo* (a kind of millet), potatoes, and vegetables, or by raising cows and goats. Although the King of Nepal has banned the traditional caste system, it continues to define the society.

Here, we briefly describe the main tribes along the Everest Highway. Other than the Sherpa tribe, most of them are found between Jiri and Shivalaya, and therefore, most of the walkers from Lukla are from the Sherpa tribe.

Brahman Tribe Belonging to the Indo-Aryan family, this tribe constitutes the priestly caste, which is the highest. Their specific duties revolve around taking charge of the many rituals. Most of the Brahmans live in the lowlands and valleys and work as farmers. They are said to have migrated into Nepal after the twelfth century, when they were driven out of the Indian plains by invading Islamic people.

Chhetri Tribe Also Indo-Aryans, the Chhetri belong to the next highest caste. They live mostly in western Nepal and are farmers. They wield political power in urban areas. For generations, most of the prime ministers, generals, bureaucrats, and high military officials in the Shah dynasty have come from this class.

Rai Tribe and Limbu Tribe These Mongoloid tribes live in mountainous areas in eastern Nepal. The Rai live between 1,000 and 2,000 meters (3,300 and 6,600 feet) altitude in a valley of the main river and tributaries of the Dudh Kosi and the Arun River. The Limbu live in the area 800 to 1,300 meters (2,600 to 4,200 feet) altitude along the Thamur River just east of the Rai tribe. The main body of Gurkha soldiers consists of four tribes: the Rai, the Limbu, the Gurung, and the Magar.

Tamang Tribe The Tamang, also belonging to the Mongoloid group, live at altitudes of about 1,500 meters (4,900 feet) in the areas stretching from the hilly terrain that surround Kathmandu into eastern Nepal.

Tibetan Tribe The Tibetans live either in the farthest part of Kali Gandaki in the high plateaus of northwestern Nepal or Dolpo, where trekking is prohibited, or in villages intermixed with the Sherpa. Their population is very small.

Sherpa Tribe The Sherpas are Tibetan Mongoloid, and their language is considered a dialect of the Tibetan language. It is said that they migrated from Tibet. Sherpa means "People of the East" in the Tibetan language. Well known as the guides and porters hired by trekking and mountain-climbing groups, they live in the Soru and Khumbu areas along the Everest Highway. Sherpas also can be found near the upper watershed of the Arun River on the south side of Makalu and the south side of the Rolwaling range. Some of the Sherpa live on Helambu on the south side of the Jugal Mountains. They also live intermixed in urban areas and mountainous villages with many different tribes who are in different occupational castes, such as the Kami, who are blacksmiths; the Sarki, who are leather workers; the Damai, who are tailors; and the Sunar, who are gold- and silversmiths.

Hinduism and Tibetan Buddhism

Hinduism is Nepal's national religion, and ninety percent of the population of Nepal is Hindu. This includes people of the highest caste, such as the Brahman, Thakur, Chhetri, and Newar, and such low-caste tribes as the Tharu, Gurun, Magar, Thakali, Tamang, Lai, and Limbu. If you start trekking from Jiri, you will experience the world of Hinduism during the three-hour walk up to Shivalaya, at villages such as those of the Brahman who live in the lowlands and valleys, and those of the Chhetri, Tamang, Rai, and Limbu.

The Hindu religion is polytheistic. There are said to be 3.3 million gods and goddesses in India, and the number increases in Nepal to 330 million. Among them, the highest gods and goddesses are Brahma, Vishnu, and Shiva. Generally, Brahma is said to have created the universe; Vishnu preserves it; and Shiva destroys it. However, Shiva and Vishnu are the most popular gods. Brahma has lost much of his popularity.

Tibetan Buddhism is the religion of the Sherpa, all Tibetans, and a portion of the Gurung tribe (Bhote in the farthest corner of Marsyangdi). Looking at the total population of Nepal, this is a small minority. Nevertheless, they are not persecuted, but rather prosper in harmony with the Hindus. You can see sacred structures of Tibetan Buddhism within Hindu temples in Kathmandu and vise versa. It is common to see members of both religions paying their respects at both buildings.

Tibetan Buddhism has two sects: the Red Cap sect, which existed before Tsongkhapa's religious reformation of the fourteenth century, and the Yellow Cap sect, which began after the reformation. Two of the high-ranking followers of Tsongkhapa were the Dalai Lama and the Panchen Lama, whose lineages have survived to the present day.

Tibetan Buddhism in the Nepal Plateau belongs to the so-called Old Style Nyingma sect, which is a branch of the Red Cap sect. Its founder was Padmasambhava. In the last half of the eighth century, he came from northwest India at the invitation of the King of Tibet, Trisong Detsen. He was a monk with strong supernatural powers. Possessing the ability to stop calamities by calling upon spirits and demons, he very quickly acquired a popular position. His other name is "Lotus Flower Birth." This is because he was taken to be a personification of Amitabha Buddha, who was born of eight lotus petals. The main statues in the front of the first floor of the *gompa* in the Khumbu district are of the Amitabha Buddha and Padmasambhava.

Tibetan Buddhism is a source of spiritual support for the Himalayan peoples, whose lives are controlled in every way by the forces of nature. The depth of their religious belief is evident when you see the Sherpas constantly chanting the sutra, "Om mani padme hum!" (O lotus-seated god of the celestial jewel!) or when you observe their humility in front of the religious objects of Tibetan Buddhism. Trekkers should be respectful when encountering such scenes.

During trekking, the major religious objects you might see are the following: *gompa* (monastery); *chorten* (stupa); *mani* stones (*mani* means "precious stone" in Sanskrit; it is a stone into which a sutra has been carved); *mendan* (a long wall of *mani* stones piled on the side of the road); *tar chen* (prayer notes with woodblock printings of sutras); *mani* wheels (a wheel in the shape of a cylinder with sutras carved on it; if you turn it once clockwise, it is like chanting the sutras a thousand times). If you encounter any of these religious objects, you should walk to their left.

Trekking Guide

From Jiri to Lukla

Day 1: Jiri to Bhandar

The Kathmandu-to-Jiri bus ticket is sold from five o'clock in the afternoon at the bus station on Durbar Marg street. Going from Jiri to Lukla usually takes six days. Porters hired at Jiri, however, usually want to have a contract to take you all the way to Namche Bazar. It is an eight-day trek, but the porters prefer to be paid for ten days.

Let's start walking toward Lukla.

From the bus's turning point at the end of Jiri, the road narrows to about 2 meters (6½ feet) wide. You come to a road on the mountainside, then to a pass, where you can look down upon the entire community of Jiri. From here you descend, cross the mountain's flanks, approach the Khimti Khola, cross a suspension bridge, and arrive at Shivalaya. It is about three hours to this point. The climb heads toward the large pass at Deurali. You emerge in the hills, where there are *tarchen, mendan,* and the like. Proceed along on the mountainside where two or three communities are located, and climb to Ghatekhola. After climbing farther into the forested area, you arrive at Deurali where many *mendan* are lined up. This is about three and a half hours from Shivalaya. On the ridge, there are also *bhatti.* You stay overnight in Bhandar / Changma, which is about a twenty-minute climb down the other side of the mountain.

Day 2: Bhandar to Seti

You walk down a small marsh, along a wide mountainside, and then, after crossing a wooden bridge, descend the steep slope in the forested area. Soon you see the community of Gholunda and the Likhu Khola below in the valley. Proceeding down a steep slope along a small marsh, you arrive at Gholunda, where *bhatti* can be found. Going down a road lined on both sides with stone fences separating it from the surrounding fields, you descend to the banks of the Likhu Khola. From there, you walk toward a suspension bridge over the upper stream, cross it, and go down the road along the left shore, arriving at the community of Likhukhola. Farther down the road along the river, you come to the Kinja Khola, a tributary. Right after crossing a suspension bridge is the village of Kinja, with about ten residences, a lodge, and a *bhatti.* It is about four hours from Bhandar.

After lunching here, a climb up 3,530-meter-high (11,649-foot-high) Lamjura La, the largest pass in the Solu region, awaits you. Since you cannot complete the climb by the end of the day, you should stay over in Seti.

Ascending the pass from Kinja, you soon arrive at Chinbu where a *bhatti* is located. The road continues to zigzag, and you should follow the mountain through the forest zone. As you look up, you see Seti. Soon you arrive at the village, which is about four and a half hours from Kinja.

Day 3: Seti to Junbesi

Ascending the road on the forested mountainside, you come out at Dhakuchu, where there are only two *bhatti.* Going a little farther up the slope using some stone steps, you arrive at Goyam, which has two *bhatti.* From here, a road starts along the ridge and passes through a forested area. The upper portion opens out, and you come to a pass where there are *mendan.* From here you traverse the mountain to the left and finally reach a *bhatti.* This is about four hours from Seti. You should probably have lunch here. After another hour's climb, you reach a pass with a *chorten.*

Heading down the slope, you enter a deep forest, which eventually opens into a village with a *bhatti.* This is Lamjura La. From here, follow the mountainside. Going from the community of Takuto, through the farm fields, you come to the beginning of the ridge and a view of Junbesi and 6,957-meter-high (22,958-foot-high) Numbur. After this, it is an easy descent to Junbesi where a *gompa* and *chorten* can be found. It is about three and a half hours from Lamjura La.

Day 4: Junbesi to Tragsindho

First you go down along the Junbesi Khola. If you want to see Thupten Chhulin, to the north, where a *gompa* (monastery) is located, climb along the river for about an hour. After passing through the village, cross a wooden bridge. Follow the bank for about five minutes, and take the road on your left. South of the main route, the road meets the Beni Khola at the lower stream of the Junbesi, and continues to Phaplu, where there is an airport. Don't miss where the routes part. To get to Tragsindho La, take the gentle tree-lined road from the juncture and follow the wide mountainside. You arrive at Solung, where there is a lodge and *bhatti.* It is about four hours from Junbesi and a good place to have lunch.

From Solung, Tragsindho La can be viewed across the Beni Khola. The road crosses a small marsh, goes over the mountain's flank, and comes down to a *bhatti.* Cross a suspension bridge over the Beni Khola, climb to Ringmo, and enter the forested area.

Soon, you come upon a cheese factory, which also serves as a lodge. Farther into the forest zone, *chorten* appear. You arrive at Tragsindho La by climbing upward. From here, Numruru, Lamjura La, and even a part of the Khumbu mountain range can be seen. When you drop down a little bit from the ridge, the *gompa* of Tragsindho can be seen. It is about a three-hour trip from Solung.

Day 5: Tragsindho to Kharikhola

Climb down the steep slope of the mountain. After taking a stone stairway between the trees and crossing a number of small marshy areas, you reach Manidingma, which you saw from Tragsindho. Go down a wide mountainside farming road until you come out at Phuleli. It takes about three and a half hours to get here, and now it is time for lunch. Going down the mountain from the village, where the farm fields continue, you arrive, in about an hour, at the banks of the Dudh Kosi. Across the suspension bridge is the village of Jubing. From here climb up to where Kharikhola starts. Steadfastly ascend the mountain road—built up here and there with stone stairways—and eventually you arrive at a ridgelike formation. The bed of the Dudh Kosi is far below, and the revered 5,761-meter-high (19,011-feet-high) Khumbila can be seen beyond the valley. Follow a flat road until you arrive at Kharikhola, a large village with lodges and a store. It is about a two-hour climb from Jubing.

Day 6: Kharikhola to Lukla

A steep slope begins immediately after you cross a suspension bridge at Kharikhola, over a stream that flows through the outskirts of the village. You arrive at Kharte, where you can find *chorten* and *bhatti*. From here, you skirt the forested areas and come to Bhukuchha and its *bhatti*. The road becomes almost flat, and you arrive at Khari La, which is the border between the Solu and Khumbu districts and affords the visitor a great view.

The road crosses one ridge after another, and soon you come to an open area, Phuiyan, where you find a *bhatti*. It takes about four hours from Kharikhola and is a good place for lunch.

From Phuiyan, the forest zone continues, and soon you arrive at the beginning of a ridge, which offers a panoramic view extending from Lukla through the Dudh Kosi valley. Upon descending into the valley, you unexpectedly come to the village of Surkhe. After passing through the village, the road diverges at the site of a small marshy area. You cross this marsh, proceed to an old road going to Phakding through Chaumrikharka. To reach Lukla, you take a stone stairway, then turn right along a small marshy area. Climbing from the back side of the marsh and going left, you zigzag to the top, where you arrive at one end of the Lukla airport runway. When you go up to the other end, you come to a village where some lodges and *bhatti* can be found. If you are coming by air from Kathmandu, then this is the beginning of your trek. It is about four hours from Phuiyan.

If you want to go from Lukla to Jiri, it is the same six-day course with the same stopovers.

From Lukla to Everest Base Camp

Day 1: Lukla to Phakding

Air tickets between Kathmandu and Lukla can be purchased at the office of the Royal Nepal Airlines, which is on the New Road in Kathmandu. During the travel season, however, it is difficult to get tickets because so many people travel by air to Lukla. Reservations should be made in advance at a travel agency in your own country or in Kathmandu before departure. Even if you can get a ticket, the airline often has to cancel its flights because of the weather, so allow extra time in your schedule for delays in both the flight there and the return trip.

Ordinarily, you should plan to take two days to travel from Lukla to Namche Bazar. The airplane from Kathmandu arrives at Lukla about ten o'clock in the morning. Two to three hours are needed to prepare for the trip, and therefore you will not depart until after lunch. The walk to Namche Bazar is uphill. Stay overnight at Phakding along the way. If you have come to Lukla by air, your trek starts here.

To get to Phakding, you walk through lodges and *bhatti* built in groups on the upper end of the runway. Outside the village, the scenery characteristic of Nepal begins as you see the houses spread across the flanks of the mountains. This is the Chaumrikharka. The old road from Surkhe enters the center of the village. At the back side of the village, you see the configuration of the V-shaped valley of the Dudh Kosi. To get to Namche Bazar, you climb beside this river.

The road descends the middle of this mountain at an easy angle and eventually meets the road from Chaumrikharka. Soon it arrives at the small community of Chapling, where six or seven houses are spread out on the flank of the mountain. There is even a *bhatti*. The road becomes flat and skirts around the mountain, where you find the next small community, Kyomma. From here, the road slopes gently downward, and you can see the flowing Dudh Kosi. You then arrive at Chumlo, where you can look up at the west peak of Kusum Kanguru, 5,579 meters (21,011 feet) high, and at the end of the valley. After another downhill walk, you reach Ghat. From here on, walk along the road lined with stone fences, climb over the saddle, and proceed along the flank of the mountain. You arrive at Phakding, which has lodges. You might want to camp in front of a *bhatti* on the other side of the suspension bridge across the Dudh Kosi, where your journey continues tomorrow. It has been about four hours from Lukla.

Day 2: Phakding to Namche Bazar

Go through the forest of pines and cedars, cross the wooden bridge, and follow the road as it winds steeply up the mountain slope past the *bhatti*. Still following the steep road, you reach Benkar, where a large *mani* stone attracts your attention.

Cross the suspension bridge at the end of the village. Take the road on the right bank of the Dudh Kosi, and go up through the forest, where a *bhatti* appears. The community located above and across the small stream is Chumoa, where there is a lodge with a sign written in Japanese saying "Inn."

After you climb for a while, you find the community of Monjo. The exit from the village has an office of the Sagarmatha National Park, where an admission fee is collected. The road goes down to the Dudh Kosi, and once you cross the suspension bridge, you are in Jorsale. This is about three and a half hours from Phakding. You might want to eat lunch here.

Outside the village is a suspension bridge. Cross it, and follow the road as it winds up steeply among the trees. Note where the Bhote Kosi, a river that starts at Nangpa La at the border, flows into the Dudh Kosi. Passing this confluence, you cross the Dudh Kosi again and begin the climb to Namche Bazar. It is about 590 meters (1,945 feet) difference in altitude. Climbing up the switchbacks along the slope, you reach the ridge called Topdhala where there is a *bhatti.* You can see the mountains of the Rolwaling range. For the first time, you are able to see Mount Everest. This is the halfway point of the climb. The remaining half, walking through conifer trees, is slightly less steep. You eventually see a row of white-walled houses and soon arrive at Namche Bazar. It has been about a four-hour walk from Jorsale.

Returning to Lukla from Namche Bazar takes a day and a half. Stay overnight at Monjo or Chumoa.

Day 3: Namche Bazar to Tengboche

Traveling from Namche Bazar to Tengboche involves descending 250 meters (825 feet), then immediately climbing up 670 meters (2,210 feet), which is physically exhausting and causes some people to experience altitude sickness. You should be very careful to monitor your physical condition.

The road comes to a saddle after climbing the east side of the mountain. You must stop at the checkpoint on the way to show your trekking permit. This can also be done on the previous day. The road levels off after crossing the east slope of the saddle. Soon thereafter you can look down the chasm of the Dudh Kosi. If you look up, you can see the whole of 6,623-meter-high (22,856-foot-high) Thamserku. The other mountains, such as Kang Taiga, at 6,685 meters (22,060 feet), and Ama Dablam, at 6,812 meters (21,480 feet), appear before you. In addition to these, Everest, Nuptse, and Lhotse can be seen at the lower end of the valley. Being surrounded by mountains heightens your sense of trekking. The road snakes around the large slopes. You see the Hotel Everest View on the top of a hill way above you. Proceed on the level road along the flank of the mountain. Looking up at the world's highest peak for a while, you find yourself in front of the *bhatti* of Sanarsa. The road now forks. The left fork is the road to Khumjung and Khumde, and to the Hotel Everest View. The middle fork is the alternate path leading to Gokyo.

To go to Tengboche, take the right fork to Sanarsa. From there proceed down to the Dudh Kosi. Cross the suspension bridge to Phunkiteng, the community located in the valley. It has been about three and a half hours from Namche Bazar. You can stop here for lunch.

After lunch, follow the steep uphill road to Tengboche. The long climb of about two and a half hours starts in the forest and gains altitude quickly, with many switchbacks on the right flank of the ridge. When you get to the top, you are in Tengboche. The mesa on the plateau has a *gompa* (destroyed by fire in January 1989 and being rebuilt) and a guest house.

Day 4: Tengboche to Pheriche

The road to Pheriche goes down stone steps from the northern end of the mesa. Soon you are in a gardenlike setting where a *mendan* stands. The village house on the left, a commune for nuns, is Deboche, otherwise called Deuche. The next community is called Miringo. Eventually, you cross a suspension bridge and climb the rocky road along the mountain. You see a single *chorten.* When you go under the *khangni* (Buddha stupa gate), you come to a big rock that can be climbed over on either side. Pangboche is just beyond this. Two roads from here lead to the left flank of the mountains. The upper road goes to the upper village where the *gompa* is being built to hold the scalp and hand bones of a yeti (abominable snowman). The level road goes to the lower village. Pangboche is the last village where people live the year round on the upper Imja Khola. Beyond this, there are some places that look like communities but are called *kharka* and are used only for summer pasturing. It has been some three and a half hours since Tengboche. You can have lunch here.

The road from the upper village, Pangboche, and the road from the lower village meet after about a ten-minute walk. The road then climbs a gentle slope along the Imja Khola and is lined with stone fences before arriving at Shomare. Another climb up to the hilly area brings you to Orsho, where there is one lone house with a *bhatti.* In fifteen minutes you are at Tsuro kharka. The road forks. The one that goes straight along the river is the alternate route leading to Dingboche and ultimately to Chhukung. To go to Pheriche, climb up the hill on the left. Standing on the ridge, you can see in the valley below a lodge and *bhatti* and also the cattle barns of a *kharka.* A climb downward brings you to Pheriche. It has been about three hours from Pangboche.

At Pheriche, there is a facility for the Himalayan Rescue Association inside the clinic run by the Tokyo Medical University. From Pheriche, symptoms of altitude sickness start to appear, and this facility can be very helpful. Since you will be continuing to Kala Pattar and Base Camp, this is a good place to adjust to the high altitude.

Heading from Pheriche to Dingboche, you can look up and see the road ascending to your right on the east slope of the mountain behind the lodge. When you climb up to the place, go to where the *chorten* is built, which looks down on the *kharka* of Dingboche. This has been one hour of travel.

Day 5: Pheriche to Lobuje

Take the sandy road in front of the *bhatti,* which remains level through the U-shaped valley, eventually arriving at the *kharka* of Phalong Karpo. A little farther ahead, the road follows the valley to the right. Another valley splits off to the left through the mountains. The route through this valley leads to Chola Tso (lake) and Chola La, 5,300 meters (17,490 feet) high, and goes over the ridge to Gokyo. The way to Lobuje climbs toward the middle of the mountain. Eventually, the road from Dingboche comes in from the right. After passing this road, go down, for a change, through an area of loose rocks and across a small stream to arrive in Tukla. At the upper part of this small stream is the Khumbu Glacier. This stream is fed by the water melting off the surface of the glacier. It has been about four hours from Pheriche. You can have lunch at either of the two *bhatti.*

When you depart Tukla, you see before you the moraine of the glacier. This climb, about 250 meters (825 feet) of nothing but uphill switchbacks, is a serious test. All trekkers going to Base Camp suffer on this steep slope. Proceed carefully, constantly keeping in mind the high altitude. Once you come to the ridge, you see a group of stones in a line commemorating people who have died. Thus ends this infamous climb. From now on, you walk on loose rocks on the flank of the mountain and cross the small stream flowing through the ablation valley. Take the road with the gentle uphill climb along the right bank. You arrive at Lobuje, where you can look up at Nuptse, to your right. It has been about four hours from Tukla. The high altitude and cold temperature make it difficult to sleep well here.

Day 6: Lobuje to Gorakshep

From Lobuje to Gorakshep usually takes only half a day, but every step gets more difficult than the last because of the altitude, which is over 5,000 meters (16,500 feet).

As you walk north on the road along the small stream, you can look back and see Taweche, at 6,501 meters (21,453 feet), and Cholotse, at 6,440 meters (21,252 feet), above the hills, familiar peaks from yesterday's travels. The ablation valley continues to slope gently. In the distance, you eventually see the triangular front of Pumo Ri, at 7,161 meters (23,631 feet), which Hillary named "Bride's Peak." In the central part of Pumo Ri, the snow stretches down before you, reaching a blackish brown hill at the bottom, where the Kala Pattar vista point, at 5,545 meters (18,298 feet), is located. The road in this ablation valley is blocked by hills, so you have to climb. You finally reach the moraine hill at the side of Changri Shar Glacier, 150 meters (495 feet) high. On top of the moraine, you see in front of you the desolate glaciers covered with rocks and sand. These are the Khumbu Glacier and Changri Nup Glacier, which comes in from the left.

The road to Gorakshep crosses the end of Changri Shar Glacier. You can hardly believe that there is a glacier under your feet, because it is covered with rocks and sand. Crossing it involves some ups and downs, and seems long. Finally, when you are atop the moraine on the opposite side, you can look down upon a *bhatti* and the glacier lake of Gorakshep, surrounded by the desolate, sandy, rocky land. You descend for about ten minutes through loose gravel. It has been about four hours from Lobuje.

If you have extra strength, climb to the summit of Kala Pattar in the afternoon. It takes about an hour and a half. The view is magnificent. The group of high summits of the Khumbu range, crowned by Mount Everest, is sublime when seen in the evening. You could say that the final goal of trekking on the Everest Highway is to enjoy the view from here.

There are two ways to climb Kala Pattar. One route approaches from the end of the ridge in the sandy area. The other starts with an abrupt climb up the flank of the mountain. Trekking time is the same. If you are planning to stay at the summit until right before sunset, don't forget to bring down clothing for protection against the cold and a flashlight for your descent.

Day 7: Gorakshep to Everest Base Camp

Normally it takes about three hours from Gorakshep to Base Camp. However, unless you really want to stay overnight there, you should not attempt more than the round-trip from Gorakshep to avoid being disabled by altitude sickness. You should stay at high-altitude locations as briefly as possible. If you have enough time, you can return as far as Lobuje. The view from Kala Pattar is much better than the one from Base Camp, where you cannot see the Everest's fine summit.

Continue along the side of the glacier lake located in an ablation valley. You soon find yourself on the side of the glacier, which is covered with rocks and muddy sand. The trace is clear because here and there cairns are piled up, so you cannot get lost. As you climb, you can see blue ice in the fissures of the glacier and forests of ice pillars. Before you, Lingtren, at 6,697 meters (22,100 feet), and Khumbutse, at 6,640 meters (21,912 feet), jut out. Going forward, as if approaching the bases of the mountains, you see the ice fall of the Western Cum tumbling in from the right. Proceed all the way to the point where you can look directly up at the ice fall. You are at Everest Base Camp, a world of rock, snow, and ice. Often you find a tent village of mountaineers who will be ascending to the top of Mount Everest.

To return to Gorakshep, you need only an hour and a half or so. From there to Namche Bazar, it is three days, staying overnight at Pheriche and Tengboche.

From Namche Bazar to Thame (Side Trip)

Although it is possible for an experienced walker to make a round-trip in one day from Namche Bazar to Thame, we describe a relaxed two-day course.

From Namche Bazar, climb past a *gompa* built on the western flank of the mountain to the top of the ridge. After that, follow the road across the flank of the mountain through tall conifer forests about 100 to 500 meters (330 to 1,650 feet) above the Bhote Kosi, which flows from the west, the direction of Thame. Eventually, in an hour or so, you arrive at Phurte, where there is a *chorten* at the entrance. To your right, you see a ridge. Cross it, and you come to a small stream. Beyond that is the community of Tesho. Going around the ridge, you soon arrive at Thamo, where there is also a *chorten* peacefully situated at the center of the village. It has been three and a half hours from Namche Bazar—time for an early lunch.

There are two roads from Thamo to Thame. The one that starts at the *chorten* in the center of the village is a new route that climbs to the upper part of the *gompa,* levels off, traverses the flank of the mountain through the upper village of Thomde, and crosses the steel bridge over the Bhote Kosi. Since we use this route on the return, we introduce another way, which goes along the river.

From Thamo, walk along the ridge for a while. You see a large *chorten* on the side of the road. Eventually, you arrive at the lower village of Thomde. There are *mendan* and *chorten,* among the many Tibetan Buddhist religious objects you can see on this road.

Looking at the small communities on the other side of the river, you walk down to the Bhote Kosi and cross the wooden bridge over the rushing stream. You start climbing a steep hill to Thame. See if you can make the climb of 200 to 250 meters (660 to 825 feet) up the steep hill without a break. Over one hill, you encounter the Thame Khola flowing down from the direction of Trashi Laptse (ridge). Cross the wooden bridge, and climb up for a while. You find yourself at one end of Thame, the lower village, surrounded by cedar trees. The houses of the village are spread out across the sandy land. One of the households runs the lodge. It has been about three hours' travel from Thamo. You can arrive by midafternoon.

The *gompa* is built on the middle of the hill north of Thame's lower village. The climb takes almost an hour along the road that rises to the left across the flank of the hill. The background is a rock wall with an overhang, under which the *gompa* is peacefully situated. From here you see the mountains of the Rolwaling range. At the farthest end is Pigphera Go Shar, at 6,730 meters (22,209 feet). To the south are mountains that are already familiar to you above the valley of the Bhote Kosi.

Returning to Namche Bazar is easily done in about four hours.

From Namche Bazar to Gokyo (Side Trip)

Day 1: Namche Bazar to Phortse Tenge through Khumjung

To climb up from Namche Bazar through Khumjung, go toward the *gompa* on the western flank of the mountain at Namche Bazar. Passing the road to Thame, climb up the steep slope behind the *gompa.* You find yourself at the upper end of Syangboche Airport. The unpaved runway has a gentle slope leading toward the valley. Near the upper end, there is even a lodge. Continuing on the mountain flank, you soon pass a road traversing up to the right. This is the road to Hotel Everest View, about forty minutes away. To get to Khumjung, proceed straight up the wide road, climbing the hill with its occasional stone steps. In no time, you are on the hill, where a *chorten* is built. Go to the ridge immediately beyond. From here you walk on level land, and you see the long line of *mendan* on the road. The school on the right is the one founded by Sir Edmund P. Hillary. A road to the left, close to the two *chorten* at the entrance of the village, brings you to Khumde in about a quarter of an hour. Going from Namche Bazar to Khumjung takes about three and a half hours.

The road to Gokyo descends from the one to Khumde. Go down the gentle slope on the stone-fenced road. After you pass the square-shaped *chorten,* climb up the stone steps built in the rock cracks. To the left is 5,761-meter-high (19,011-foot-high) Khumbila. If you go straight down, you arrive at Sanarsa. When you stand on the eastern side of the mountain, you are looking down upon the *bhatti* at Sanarsa on the banks of the Dudh Kosi. The narrow road continues under the rock cliff, then slopes gently along the mountainside and is joined by the road from Sanarsa. Eventually, you are looking up at the *chorten* of Moung La at the saddle of the mountain ahead of you. It is about three hours' travel from Khumjung to Moung La. There is a *bhatti* to the side of the *chorten.* You can eat lunch here. After this, go straight down to the Dudh Kosi while you are being gazed upon by rocky peaks way above your head to your left. You are now in Phortse Tenge, where you camp today. On the way to Phortse Tenge, there is a *bhatti.* If you did not bring a tent, we recommend that you spend the night here. From Khumjung to Phortse Tenge is an hour and a half.

Day 2: Phortse Tenge to Machhermo

The road to Machhermo is on the left bank of Dudh Kosi. Climb the steep slope through the woods, up to the rhododendron glens. From there on, the road is a gentle climb. Eventually, you are looking through the birch trees up at Cho Oyu, 8,201 meters (27,063 feet) high. A large waterfall is on your left. Soon, you arrive at a lone *kharka* at Tongba, at timberline. Go around the *kharka,* climb up, and you are on the open area of the mountainside. Proceed around the ridge and keep climbing. Cross another ridge and you find yourself in Dole. It has been about four hours from Phortse Tenge. Have lunch here.

From Dole, climb up the mountain flank facing you, then cross three ridges. You arrive at Luza. Crossing still another ridge, you can look at Machhermo in the wide valley. At the farthest end of the valley, you see Kyajo Ri, 6,186 meters (20,414 feet) high, its sharp peak towering high in the sky. It has been about three hours from Dole.

Day 3: Machhermo to Gokyo

Start by taking the road up the mountainside in front of you. Stand on the top of the ridge, then go down the gentle slope to Panka. Before you are the mountains towering high on the country's border, such as Cho Oyu, Ngojumba Kang, and

Gyachung Kang. The tail of Ngojumba Glacier is just ahead. To the east, the peaks of Cholotse and Taweche stand tall.

Go down to the water emerging from Panka and you are at the end of the glacier. Proceed down the steep, loose gravel slope to the hilly area, then to the rocky road, crossing the wooden bridge, and climb up all the way to the end of the rocky area. You are standing at the edge of the glacier. The road levels off as it passes through an ablation valley. Soon, you arrive at the first lake, Tso Mengma, and then at the second lake, Tso Paluma. Walk down the road along the small stream. When you can see the grand view, you are looking at the Dudh Pokhari (Tso Rangma), with the lake at Gokyo lying in front of you. Walk about ten minutes or so on the eastern side of the lake and you see a ***kharka.*** This is your goal, Gokyo. It is about five hours from Machhermo. You can reach it about noon.

The highlight at Gokyo is the view from Gokyo summit, which you can climb to within three hours. The 360-degree panorama is no less beautiful than the one from Kala Pattar. To get to Gokyo Peak, walk on the stepping-stones in the small stream flowing into the northern end of the lake. You see a path to the ridge over your head. The path is steep and clear at first, but after passing the grassy area it becomes merely a trace. On the upper part, you may have to pick your way among the rocks to reach the summit. From the long, narrow Gokyo Peak with huge rocks sprinkled here and there, you can see Cho Oyu to the north and, as you look east, the mountains at the Nepal-Tibet border, such as Ngojumba Kang, Gyachung Kang, Chantse, Everest, and Lhotse. To the far east, Makalu stands up high in the sky. You can also see the extraordinarily long Ngojumba Glacier before you. East of the glacier are the mountains of the Khumbu range, such as Cholotse, Taweche, Ama Dablam, and Thamserku, all over 6,000 meters (19,800 feet). As at Kala Pattar, the climax occurs with the evening view. If you intend to stay until sunset at the top of the summit, be sure to bring along some down clothing and a flashlight.

The journey down from Gokyo to Namche Bazar is a two-day trip, staying over at Dole on the way.

From Namche Bazar to Chhukung (Side Trip)

Day 1: Namche Bazar to Tengboche
Day 2: Tengboche to Dingboche

For the directions to Chhukung, please see the route from Lukla to Everest Base Camp as far as Tsuro.

From Tsuro to Dingboche, go straight on the road along the Imja Khola, past the climb north to Pheriche. Soon you cross a wooden bridge over the water, which flows down from the direction of Pheriche. Cimb up the steep slope and stay on the loose gravel road. Go to the top of the hill and follow the road while you look down at the Imja Khola. The valley starts to open up in front of you and a line of ***mendan*** appears. You also see a ***kharka*** at Dingboche. It is seven hours from Tengboche and about one hour from Tsuro.

Day 3: Dingboche to Chhukung

Proceed along the stone-fenced road with fields on both sides. Pass the ***kharka*** of Dingboche and descend to the beach on the left bank of the Imja Khola, where you see ***mani*** stones. The road continues into the hills on the left. After you cross the hills and a small stream flowing down from the craggy mountains on the left, continue on the road, which now is loose stones, up the hill. You arrive at the ***kharka*** of Bibre where there are five or six cow sheds. It is about one and a half hours from Dingboche.

From Bibre, follow the road across the flank of the mountain for quite some time. Go to the sandy area below on the right, and proceed through a field of big stones. You cannot get lost, since this is the only road. Eventually, you cross the rock field at the base of Nuptse Glacier, where giant rocks are piled on each other. Cross the wooden bridge over a stream flowing down from the glacier, again entering a rocky area. Cross the additional two small streams. Then, you still have to cross the Imja Khola, which is 4 to 5 meters (13 to 16½ feet) wide here. If the water is high, finding the stepping-stones in the stream may entail some effort. Then climb up the moraine hill without stopping. A ***kharka*** appears, and you are in Chhukung. It is about two and a half hours from Bibre and four hours from Dingboche. Two lodges are available.

Chhukung is the farthest ***kharka*** on the Imja Khola. Looking west, you see Numbur and the Rolwaling range standing tall. To the south are Ama Dablam and Kang Leyamu; to the north, the huge rock wall from Lhotse to Nuptse.

There is a road from Chhukung to 6,160-meter-high (20,328-foot-high) Imja Tse (Island Peak) or to the base camp at the south wall of Lhotse. There are no ***bhatti*** beyond this point, and you cannot stay overnight unless you bring a tent. Even if your Sherpa knows the route, try to make this a day trip. If you are affected by the altitude, it is safer to return.

Climbing down from Chhukung to Namche Bazar is a two-day trip, staying overnight at Tengboche.

Sources of Information

• Kathmandu Trekking Agencies

Adventure Nepal Trekking Pvt., Ltd.
Keshar Mahal, Kathmandu, GPO Box 915, TEL: 411453

Ama Dablam Trekking Pvt., Ltd.
Lazimpat, Kathmandu, GPO Box 3035, TEL: 410219

Anapurna Mountaineering & Trekking Pvt., Ltd.
Durbar Marg, Kathmandu, GPO Box 795, TEL: 222999

Chomolhari Trekking Pvt., Ltd.
Durbar Marg, Kathmandu, GPO Box 1519, TEL: 222422

Cosmo Trek Pvt., Ltd.
Hotel Shangri La, Lazimpat, Kathmandu, GPO Box 2541, TEL: 412595

Everest Express Tours & Travels Pvt., Ltd.
Durbar Marg, Kathmandu, GPO Box 482, TEL: 220759

Everest Trekking Pvt., Ltd.
Kamaladi, Kathmandu, GPO Box 1676, TEL: 220558

Everest Trekking Pvt., Ltd.
Naxal, Kathmandu, GPO Box 339, TEL: 413017

Gorkha Treks Pvt., Ltd.
Lainchour, Kathmandu, GPO Box 4503, TEL: 413806

Himalayan Horizons Pvt., Ltd.
Thamel, Kathmandu, GPO Box 4047, TEL: 223266

Himalayan Journeys Pvt., Ltd.
Kantipath, Kathmandu, GPO Box 989, TEL: 226138,
Trek Operation Office: Naxal, Kathmandu, TEL: 413032, 410836

Himalayan Shangri La Treks Pvt., Ltd.
Durbar Marg, Kathmandu, GPO Box 221, TEL: 413303, 222160

International Trekkers Pvt., Ltd.
Hitty Durbar, Kathmandu, GPO Box 1273, TEL: 224157, 220594

Jai Himal Trekking Pvt., Ltd.
Durbar Marg, Kathmandu, GPO Box 3017, TEL: 221707, 224248

Lama Excursions Pvt., Ltd.
Durbar Marg, Kathmandu, GPO Box 2056, TEL: 220940

Last Frontiers Trekking Pvt., Ltd.
Lainchaur, Kathmandu, GPO Box 881, TEL: 414512

Mountain Travel Pvt., Ltd.
Naxal, Kathmandu, GPO Box 170, TEL: 414508

Rover Treks & Expedition (P), Ltd.
Naxal, Nagpokhari, Kathmandu, GPO Box 1081, TEL: 414373

Sherpa Cooperative Trekking (P), Ltd.
Durbar Marg, Kathmandu, GPO Box 1338, TEL: 414416, 223348

Sherpa Trekking Service Pvt., Ltd.
Kamaladi, Kathmandu, GPO Box 500, TEL: 222489

Trans Himalayan Trekking Pvt., Ltd.
Durbar Marg, Kathmandu, GPO Box 283, TEL: 223854, 223871

• Air Service between Kathmandu and Lukla

Royal Nepal Airlines Corporation
Kantipath, Kathmandu, GPO Box 410
Domestic: Thapathali, Kathmandu, TEL: 220757, 214491

• Bus Service between Kathmandu and Jiri

Amiko Yatayat Sema Samitee Bus Park
Kathmandu, TEL: 216497

• Official Organizations

United States Embassy
Pani Pokhri, Kathmandu, TEL: 411179

Central Immigration Office
Maitideri, Kathmandu, TEL: 412337

Tourist Information Center
Basantapur, Kathmandu, TEL: 220818
Tribhuvan International Airport, Kathmandu, TEL: 410537

• Hospitals

Bir Hospital, Kantipath, Kathmandu, TEL: 411550
Maternity Hospital, Thapathali, Kathmandu, TEL: 214205
Nepal Eye Hospital, Tripuresshwor, Kathmandu, TEL: 213317
Patan Hospital, Lagankhel, Laritpur, TEL: 521034

Daily Conversation in Nepali

Shoji Takezawa

1. Good morning. Good day.
   Good evening.
   Namaste.
2. Glad to meet you.
   Tapainglai bhettera dhere khushi laagyo.
3. What is your name?
   Tapaingko naam ke ho?
4. My name is Tom.
   Mero naam thaam ho.
5. How are you?
   Tapainglai sangchai hunuhun chha?
6. Fine, thank you.
   Ma sangchai chhu.
7. Thank you very much.
   Dhanyabaad.
8. Are you fine, too?
   Tapainglai pani?
9. Where do you come from?
   Kahaambaatt aunubho?
10. I come from America.
    Amerika baat aaen.
11. When did you come to Kathmandu (here)?
    Kaatthmanddu maa (yahaa) kahile aunubho?
12. I came yesterday.
    Hijo aaen.
13. (to a person passing by)
    Excuse me.
    Chhemaa garnos.
14. Yes, what is it?
    Bhannos?
15. Where is the — hotel?
    — hottel kahan chha?
16. Which direction is it?
    Kataa parchha?
17. It is north.
    Uttarmaa.
18. Are you going there?
    Tapaing chahan jaane?
19. Yes.
    Ho.
20. Then, let's go together.
    Usobhae masang jaaunglaa.

Continued

21. Can I stay at this hotel?
Ma ehi hottelmaa basna chaahanchhu?
22. Is there a shower / bathing room?
Nuhaune kotthaa chha?
23. How much is it for an overnight stay?
Ek dinko kati parchha?
24. What is the room number?
Kati nambarko kothaa maa?
25. Please clean up the room.
Kothaa maa saaf garnos.
26. Where is the toilet?
Ttoilett kataa chha?
27. What time are we going?
Kati bajye jaane?
28. At seven o'clock in the morning?
Bihaanko saat bajye?
29. Which way are we going?
Kataa tera jaane?
30. To the east.
Purbatera
31. How far from here to —?
Yahaabaatt — kati ttaaddhaa chha?
32. About five or six *kos*.
Karib paanch chha kos jati.
33. Let's go slowly.
Bistaarai jaaunglaa.
34. Come after me / follow me.
Mero pachhi aaunos.
35. Where is this? Where is this place?
Yo kun tthaun ho?
36. Is this the right way to go to —?
— jaane baatto etaa tik chha?
37. Please draw a map for going to —.
— jaane naksha lekidinos.
38. What is its name?
Tyasko naam keraa ho?
39. Its name is kera (banana).
Esko naam keraa ho.
40. What is this?
Yo ke ho?
41. That is a mango.
Tyo aanp ho.
42. How much is this?
Esko mol kati ho?
43. Two for one and a half rupee.
Duittaa tin mol.
44. That is very expensive.
Dherai mahaango chha.
45. Please discount it a little.
Thorai sasto garnos.
46. Please give me four of them.
Chaarwattaa dinos.
47. Where can I get kerosene?
Mattitel kahaan paainchha?
48. Does the bus to — come here?
Ke yahaan jaane bas aaunchha?
49. Yes, it does.
Ho, aaunchha.
50. Does this bus go to —?
Yo bas — maa jaane?
51. No, it does not.
Hoina, na jaane.
52. Which bus goes to —?
— maa jaane bas hun ho?
53. Please say it one more time.
Feri bhannos.
54. I understand.
Thaahaa chha.
55. What happened?
Ke bhayo?
56. I have a headache (stomachache).
Kapaal (pett) dukhyo.
57. I have caught a cold.
Rugaa laagekochha.
58. I have a fever.
Jaddo chha.
59. I am thirsty.
Thirkhaa laagyo.
60. Please wait a moment.
Ekaichin parkhanos.
61. Let's go have tea.
Chiyaa piune jaaungla.
62. Where are we going?
Kaan jaane?
63. To the teahouse nearby.
Chheumaa chaai dokaansamma.
64. Do you take sugar in your coffee?
Kafi maa chini haalne?
65. Yes, please add sugar and milk.
Ho. Chini ra dudh haalnos.
66. Don't add a lot of sugar.
Dherai chini na haal ni.
67. Nepali food is delicious.
Nepaali khaanaa mittho chha.
68. Have you had a meal?
Bhaat khaanubho?
69. I have eaten.
Khaaen.
70. Where is the menu?
Menyu kahaan chha?
71. How much is a plate of food?
Ek plettko kati?
72. See you again.
Feri bhettaunglaa.
73. Good-bye.
Bidaa chha.

• Useful Vocabulary

Address = tthegaanaa
Bad = karaab
Beautiful = sundar
Big = tthulo
Boy = kettaa
Bridge = pul
Buy = kin
Cloud = baada
Cold (climate) = jaaro
Cold (object) = chiso
Come = aau
Cook = pakaau
Do = gar
Drink = piu
Eat = khaa
Egg = ful
Enjoyable = ramailo
Expensive = maahaango
Family = pariwaar
Far = taaddhaa
Fast = chhitho
Father = baab
Girl = ketti
Give = di
Go = jaa
Good = raamro
Green vegetable = saag
Hear = sun
Hill = chuchuro
Inexpensive = sasto
Lake = taal
Liquor = rakshi
Long = laamo
Look for = khoj
Make = banaau
Map = nakshaa
Meat = maasu
Medicine = ausadhi
Milk = dudh
Mother = aamaa
Mountain = ddaanro
Name = naam
Near = najik
Oil = tel
Older brother = daaju
Older sister = didi
Pond = pokhari
Rain = paani
Rice = chaamal
River = nadi
Road, path = baatto
Rock = chattaan
Salt = nun
Salty = nunilo
Say = bhan
Seasoning = masalaa
See = her
Sell = bech
Sew = siu
Short = chhotto
Sleep = sut
Slow = dilo
Small = saano
Soap = saabun
Speak = bol
Spicy hot = piro
Sugar = chini
Sweet = guliyo
Take = li
Tasty = mittho
Temple = mandir
Tent = paal
Towel = rumaal
Tree = rukh
Wake up = utth
Walk = ghum
Water = paani
Wife = swaasni
Wind = haawaa
Write = lekh
Younger brother = bhaai
Younger sister = baahini

• Time Expressions

One hour = ek ghanttaa
One o'clock = ek baje
One minute = ek minett
15 minutes past = sawaa
It is 15 minutes past one o'clock = Sawaa ek baje.
30 minutes = saaddhe
It is 1:30 = Saaddhe ek baje.
15 minutes before = paune
It is 15 minutes before two o'clock = Paune dui baje.

• Quantitative Expressions

kos = a unit of distance equal to about 3 kilometers. There is a resting place set up every *kos*. One day's trek runs 4 *kos*. *Keji* is a descriptive way of saying kilogram. In rural areas, traditional units like *daarni* (about 2.5 kilograms), *ser* (about 800 grams), and *paau* (about 200 grams) are used. *Gaj* is a unit of length equal to about 91 centimeters. It is about the same length as an adult's arms stretched open from fingertip to fingertip, or about three paces.

• Numbers

1 = ek	9 = nau
2 = dui	10 = das
3 = tin	20 = bis
4 = chaar	25 = pachchis
5 = paach	30 = tis
6 = chha	50 = pachaas
7 = saat	100 = sae = ek sae
8 = aatth	1,000 = ek hajaar

One thing = euttaa
Two things = duittaa
Three things = tin ttaa
Four things = chaar wattaa
For all subsequent numbers used in counting things, just add *wattaa* to the number.

• Days of the Week

Sunday = aitabaar
Monday = sombaar
Tuesday = manggalbaar
Wednesday = budhabaar
Thursday = bihibaar
Friday = shukrabaar
Saturday = shanibaar

• Directions

East = purba
Left = baayaan
North = uttar
Right = daayaan
South = dakkhin
West = pashchim

• Miscellaneous Expressions

Breakfast = bihaanko khaanaa
Dinner = belukaako khaanaa
Early morning = saberai bihaan
Evening = belukaa
Lunch = diungsoko khaanaa
Midnight = madhyeraat
Morning = bihaan
Night = raat
Noon = diungso
Now = ab
Today = aaj
Tomorrow = bholi
Twilight = sangjh
Yesterday = hijo

• How to Use Nouns

1. Noun + ho = — is. It is —.
   It is a book = Pustak ho.
2. Noun + hoina = It is not —.
   It is not a book = Pustak hoina.
3. Noun + chha = There is / are —. — exist(s).
   There is a book (there are books) = Pustak chha.
4. Noun + chhaina = There is / are not —. — do / does not exist.
   There is / are not book(s) = Pustak chhaina.
5. Noun + ko = —'s. of —. Possessive.
   Schoolbook = paatthashalaako pustak.
   Fish tail = maachhaako puchchhar.
6. Noun + maa = In, on, at —.
   Bird in a tree = rukhmaa charaa
7. Noun + baata = from — (place)
   Came from school = paatthashalaabaat aaeko

• How to Use Verbs

1. Verb stem + ne = normal polite verb form in the present tense
   Go = jaane. Come = aaune.
2. Verb stem + nos = Please —.
   Please go = Jaanos. Please come = Aaunos.
3. Verb stem + nuparchha = have to —. must —.
   Have to go = jaanuparchha. Have to come = aaunuparchha.

• How to Use Adjectives

1. Adjective + Noun = noun modification
   Big book = tthulo pustak
2. Adjective + chha = adjectival predicate
   Is big = tthulo chha
3. Adjective + chhaaina = negative adjectival predicate
   Is not big = tthulo chhaaina

• Demonstratives, Interrogatives, Expressions of Degree

This one = yo
That one = tyo
That one over there = u
This = esko
That = tyesko
Where = kaan
Here = jaan
That place over there = tyaan
(Toward) which way = kataa
(To) this place = etaa
(To) that place over there = tyetaa
When = kahile
How much / many = kati
This much / many = eti
A few, a little = thorai
A lot = dherai

• Monetary Expressions

Money = paisaa
Price = mol
One rupiya = ek rupiyaan
One paisa = ek paisaa
One-quarter rupi = ek sukaa
  25 paisaa = 1 sukaa. 75 paisaa = tin sukaa = 3 sukaa.
  Maximum is 9 sukaa, or 2.25 rupiyaan.
One-half rupiyaan = ek mohar
  50 paisaa make 1 mohar. 3 rupiyaa = chaa mohar = 6 mohar.
  Maximum is 9 mohar, or 4.5 rupiyaan.

Sounds of the Nepali Language

The sounds of Nepali range from those that are familiar to speakers of English to others that are completely different from any sounds found in European languages. Before beginning your foray into Nepali conversation, take a few minutes to familiarize yourself with the following approximations of the sounds of the language. Keep in mind that the following spellings of sounds and words are English transliterations only. Traditionally, Nepali, like Sanskrit and Hindi, is written in the Devanagari alphabet.

Single Vowels

a	a very short sound, something like the *u* in *but*
aa	a longer sound, like the *a* in *mark*
e	a slightly longer version of the *e* in *west*
i	a slightly longer version of the *i* in *sizzle*
o	like the *o* in *morning*
u	another short sound, similar to the *u* in *put*

Diphthongs

ai	like the *ai* in *aisle*
au	like the *ow* in *cow,* never as in *August*

All Nepali vowels can be nasalized, as in French. For the most part, such nasalization is noted in the transliterated conversation lesson by placing an *m, n,* or *ng* after the vowel.

Consonants

b	similar to the English *b*
bh	an aspirated *b,* made by blowing a puff of air out with the *b* sound
ch	similar to the English *ch* in *chin,* but with less breath
chh	an aspirated, breathy *ch,* something like the second *ch* in *church*
d	similar to the English *d*
dh	an aspirated version of *d*
dd	a retroflex *d* made by touching the tip of the tongue against the roof of the mouth while making the *d* sound
ddh	an aspirated retroflex *d.* This sound combines two very unfamiliar vocalizations and clearly takes a bit of time to get right. Add a puff of air to touching the roof of your mouth while saying *d.*
f	a strong, slightly longer version of the English *f,* like saying *fffight*
g	similar to the English *g* as in *gown,* never as in *gem*
gh	an aspirated breathy *g*
h	a strongly sounded *h*
j	similar to the English *j* as in *jam*
jh	an aspirated breathy version of *j*
k	similar to the English *k* as in *ski,* with very little breathiness
kh	an aspirated, breathy *k* as in *keep*
l	similar to the English *l* as in *lilt*
m	similar to the English *m* as in *milk*
n	similar to the English *n* as in *neat*
ng	similar to the English *nn* as in *singer*
p	similar to the English *p* as in *spit,* with very little breathiness
ph	an aspirated, breathy *p* as in *peace,* never as in *phone*
r	slightly trilled as in Spanish
s	similar to the English *s* as in *silk*
sh	similar to the English *sh* as in *sheet*
t	similar to the English *t* as in *stick,* with very little breathiness
th	an aspirated, breathy *t* as in *tire,* never as in *them*
tt	a retroflex version of *t,* said with the tongue tip at the roof of the mouth and with very little breathiness
tth	an aspirated retroflex *t*
w	similar to the English *w* as in *well* or *low*
y	similar to the English *y* as in *yes,* never as in *lying*
z	a softer *z* sound than in English, but otherwise similar

AFTERWORD

I traveled to Nepal some thirty times over ten years. The first route I walked was the Everest Highway, as a member of the Lhotse South Wall Climbing Group.

I gathered the information for this book during six trips from 1985 to 1989. Nepal is a society where your appearance is important. The host of the inn where I stayed the first time and the villagers I talked with remembered my face when I visited again, and they welcomed me. The more often I met them, the more they showed a friendliness that was like the way they treated their relatives. Photographing the people became possible only when we got to know one another. Before then, whenever I readied my camera to take a picture, they immediately averted their faces.

Whenever I visited the homeland of the Sherpa, I was impressed by their serious and deeply held devotion to Tibetan Buddhism, and the richness in their hearts, which I saw expressed in their smiles, unfailing despite their poverty. I, who kept observing their lives through a viewfinder, was also always being observed by them. Once again, I had to admit that human beings are drawn to other human beings, no matter what their unique point of view might be.

Ryōhei Uchida